FROM
OPTION
To
OPENING

THIRD EDITION, REVISED

FROM
OPTION
To
OPENING

THIRD EDITION, REVISED

DONALD C. FARBER

DRAMA BOOK SPECIALISTS (PUBLISHERS)
NEW YORK

© Copyright 1968, 1970, 1977 by Donald C. Farber

Third Edition, Revised

Library of Congress Cataloging in Publication Data

Farber, Donald C
  From option to opening.

    1.Theater—Production and direction.
2. Off-Broadway theater. I. Title.
PN2291.F3   1977   792'.02   76-58845
ISBN 0-910482-80-2

Printed in the United States of America

f o r . . .

Annie

Patty

Seth

(In Alphabetical Order, naturally)

I want to express my special thanks to RALPH PINE *of Drama Book Specialists (Publishers) for his patient, knowledgeable, understanding assistance and his helpful suggestions.*

I also want to thank friends
Norman Kean, David Bishop, Craig Belknap, Virginia Kahn and Linda Readerman for their helpful assists.

Preface to the Third Edition

The first edition of this book was published in 1968 when off-Broadway was flourishing. In 1970 a second revised edition was published and off-Broadway was still in business, but would soon be winding down.

It is interesting to note that the production budget for a 199 seat theatre for a straight play in the first edition was $23,000.00; in the second edition, $32,000.00; if that same play were to be produced today, its budget would probably be in the vicinity of $50,000.00. A musical budget reproduced in the first edition for a 299 seat theatre was $40,000.00; in the second edition, $55,000.00; the same play produced today would probably be in the neighborhood of between $125,000.00 and $150,000.00.

It is also interesting to note that the longest running show in the history of our country, with which I am closely associated, is a small musical which was financed in 1960 for a total of $16,500.00.

FROM OPTION TO OPENING

I have been asked a number of times by persons anxious to get a copy of *From Option to Opening* why there has not been a third edition. My answer has always been that "we are out of print because off-Broadway is 'out of print.' "

I have since discovered that this book has been used not only by off-Broadway producers and would-be producers but also extensively by persons interested in off-off-Broadway, professional (and non-professional) Resident Theatre, Dinner-Theatre, Stock, Amateur and Community Theatre, as well as a very wide assortment of theatre buffs. The basics set forth in the book originally with respect to off-Broadway are basics applicable to all theatre in all parts of our country. Acquisition of rights, coproduction agreements, the producing entity, the Limited Partnership Agreement, the SEC, raising money, the theatre agreement, etc. are basic theatre business which should be understood by all in the industry.

So, although the book was originally written for off-Broadway, we have discovered that its use has been much broader. It appeared feasible and advisable to have a third edition since there was a continuing demand for it from numerous people throughout the country.

Having decided to do a third edition of this book, I was faced with two possibilities.

I could rewrite the book, update all contract terms concerning dollar amounts and change every reference to off-Broadway so that it would be specifically applicable to other productions as well. This alternative would have involved a huge amount of work, delayed publication and substantially increased the book's price. This option would also have meant that it would have ended up a different book and I was very satisfied with it the way it was.

The second option was to republish the book as it is, call your attention to the fact that certain dollar amounts are different in some contracts today and also point out that what the book contains is applicable to all theatre everywhere—except to some extent a Broadway production, which has more specific contractual and union limitations applicable to it.

I opted for the second possibility because I did not really want to see plastic surgery performed on what remains my favorite of the books I have written. In doing this I have included new budgets typical of a current off-Broadway production, an off-off-Broadway production company and a professional Resident Community theatre. But bear in mind that there have been some changes in the dollar amounts of the union contracts discussed. This is a continuing problem however, since even if those constantly variable terms had been updated they could become outdated soon afterwards.

You may easily communicate with any respective union to obtain an updated contract. The budgets added are current budgets and reflect any changes to date. The basics set forth in this book are indeed "basics" and as I said are applicable to most theatre.

I hope this book contributes to your better understanding of the theatre business and I do hope that it brings you as much pleasure as it has brought me.

Donald C. Farber
New York City, 1976

Contents

Introduction   **1**

1   Optioning a Property   **6**

Warranties and Representations   7
Length of Option   7
Option Cost   8
Play Cost (Royalties)   9
What the Option Buys   11
What an Option Conditionally Buys   11
     right to tour   11
     english production   14
     right to move to broadway   15
     subsidiary rights   16
Billing Credits   22
House Seats   23
Authors' Approvals   24
Arbitration   24
Assignability of Option   24
Option of First Refusal   25
Buyers' Market   25
Typical Option (Example)   26
Adaptations   32
     basic work—copyright ownership   33

royalties for basic work   33
basic work option fee   33
the adapter   34

2   Co-Production Agreements   **35**

Front Money   37
Joint Venture Agreement (Example)   38
Associate Producer—Money   41

3   The Producing Company   **43**

Partnership or Corporation   44
limited liability   44
tax benefits   44
Corporation As a Partner   45
The Limited Partnership   46
how and what is limited   46
legal publication   47
assignments   48
Limited Partnership Agreement Form   49
profit sharing   49
budget-capitalization   50
abandonment   51
payment of profits   51
return of profits to company   52
producer's fee and cash office charge   52
bonds and bond deals   53
overcall and loans   56
option provisions in agreement   56
termination of partnership   57
miscellaneous   57

4   Raising the Money   **59**

Budgets   59
Typical Budgets (Examples)   61
Dramatic Play Production Budget 199 Seat Theatre   62
Dramatic Play Weekly Operating Budget 199 Seat
    Theatre   64
Off-Broadway Musical Production Budget   66
Off-Broadway Musical Operating Budget   68
Backers' Auditions   70

The Securities and Exchange Commission 72
Offering Circular (Example) 76
The Attorney General 83
Investment Procedure 84
Starting the Company 84

5 Obtaining a Theatre **86**

Advance Deposit 87
Four Wall Contract 87
Lease or License 88
Run of the Show—Moving 88
Stop Clause 89
Payment of Rent 89
Theatre License and Rehearsals 90
Equity Requirements 90
Maintenance and Concessions 90
Advertising 91
Removal at End and House Seats 91
Insurance 91
Assignability 92
Location 92
Bargaining 93
Variety of Theatres 93

6 Cast, Crew and Personnel **94**

The Director 94
The Stage Manager 97
The Cast 97
The Actors' Equity Association Contract 98
Sets, Costumes and Lights 99
Press Agent 101
Advertising Agency 101
General Manager 101
Company Manager 102
Accountants and Accountings 103
Attorney 104

7 Musicals **105**

Original Cast Album 106
Publisher 108

Musicians 108
Arrangements 108
Choreographer 109
Musical Director 110

8 Rehearsals, Open, Run or Close 111

Rehearsals 112
Previews 113
Opening Night 113
Reviews 113
Party 114
After Opening Night 115
Scaling the House, Twofers, Discount Tickets 117

9 Repertories, Children's Theatre, Off-Off and Resident Professional Theatre 119

Repertory Company 119
Children's Theatre 121
Off-Off-Broadway 122
Resident Professional Theatre 124

10 Vitally Important Odds and End 125

The Art of Negotiation 125
Conflicts of Interest 128
Package Deals 130
The League of Off-Broadway Theatres and Producers 130
Ethics—Honesty 131
Good Producing 132
Middle Theatres 133
Off-Off-Broadway Theatre Budget 135
Resident Theatre Company Budget 138
Resident Theatre Company Budget for Shakespearean
    Student Audience Program 140
Estimated Production Budget for 499 Seat Theatre
    (Middle Theatre) 141
Estimated Weekly Operating Budget for 499 Seat
    Theatre (Middle Theatre) 143

Introduction

Off-Broadway producing is a business. In fact, it has become an important part of the business that there is no business like. It's difficult to measure the influence that off-Broadway has had on our theatre. We do know, of course, that many of our important stars and prominent playwrights were first discovered in off-Broadway productions. The influence of off-Broadway extends even further, however, as off-Broadway productions have actually influenced the direction and development of our theatre.

"I think it's not good enough for a Broadway production, so it probably should be done off-Broadway." What a gross error to assume that a play must be so good for Broadway and something less good for off-Broadway.

There are distinctions between what should be done on Broadway and what should be done off-Broadway, but it has nothing to do with the quality of the show. There are, for example, different markets. Some people will patronize Broadway shows who would never patronize an off-Broadway show until it is a smash hit. The theatre party groups are partial to Broadway productions. The expense account executive entertains his out-of-town guests at a Broadway show. The student and progressive thinker may patronize an experimental off-Broadway production. Usually off-Broadway tickets are cheaper so persons on a limited budget may think twice before they spend close to $15 for a Broadway show, but will only think once about spending half that amount for an off-Broadway show. Some productions fare better in intimate surroundings. There are no intimate Broadway theatres in the same sense that the less than 299 seat theatres are intimate.

Of course it costs many times as much to produce a Broadway show than it does to produce an off-Broadway show. This in and of itself should not be the determining factor as to where you produce the play, for I am told by my producer clients that it's just as easy or just as hard to raise $200,000 to produce a good Broadway production as it is to raise $40,000 to do a good off-Broadway production.

There are, of course, numerous other distinctions which will be helpful in determining where you wish to produce a given play. However, by all means, don't let the degree of "good" be the determining factor. If it isn't good, don't do it on or off Broadway.

A successful off-Broadway producer must have the unique combination of good creative judgment, taste, and business sense. Coupled with these qualities he must be in a position to raise capital for something in which he believes. The rewards for an off-Broadway producer can be large quantities of money, but this by itself is rarely enough incentive to result in a totally satisfactory production. There may be esthetic rewards which come from doing something one believes in, in a particular way.

How do you start? How do you get the answers to the numerous questions that will confront you and plague you? Are you even aware of the questions which will need answering? I suspect that one could start working as an usher off-Broadway, work himself into the position of treasurer of the box-office, and know a lot of things about how a production is handled without really knowing what the job of producing a theatrical play consists of. There are no schools teaching the hard facts of off-Broadway life, and if you think that this book, or any book, will give you all of the answers to all of the problems, save your time and read no further. No book can be the substitute for countless man hours of experience. Although you may not learn all of the answers from this book, you may at least learn about some of the problems that you will be confronted with when you do start producing your off-Broadway show. You will have to seek help and guidance with the answers, but at least you will better understand the problems, and perhaps know in which direction to look for the answers.

Before proceeding further, we really ought to have some idea of what we mean by "off-Broadway." Actors' Equity Association's definition (which is accepted by the Dramatists Guild, Inc. by reference to the Actors' Equity Minimum Basic Contract) is perhaps as good as any, especially since their definition will apply to all contracts dealing with actors. Off-Broadway is defined as the Borough of Manhattan outside the area bounded by Fifth and Ninth Avenues, from 34th Street to 56th Street, and by Fifth Avenue to the Hudson River from 56th Street to 72nd Street. An off-Broadway theatre, in addition to being outside that area, is not more than 299 seats.

Just a word on the uniqueness of the off-Broadway theatre scene before we start tackling the problems. It can be noted that off-Broadway producing is unlike anything else in the world. If you are producing a Broadway show, in most areas there are some standards, certain well defined, previously-defined limits to your contractual experiences. In the off-Broadway arena, the contractual arrangements are less well defined. For an example, if you are optioning a Broadway script, the Dramatists Guild, Inc. Minimum Basic Production Contract which has been negotiated and renegotiated, will provide your basic terms. Albeit this contract is amended in every instance with certain clauses being added, but nevertheless the basic agreement is there, and any amendments to it will require the Dramatists Guild, Inc. approval. Not so off-Broadway, as we shall shortly see, the range of option terms is as variable as one might imagine. It is for this reason that one should, if one does not know the answers, at least know the problems.

There are, at the present time, negotiations being carried on between the Dramatist Guild Inc. and the League of off-Broadway Theatres and Producers. It is always a possibility that a standard Option agreement will result from the meetings.

You will of necessity, in some instances, as a producer, be confronted with legal problems and legal documents. It is intended that to the extent possible, these problems will be discussed for you in non-legal language as it is a recognized fact that most off-Broadway producers are not attorneys. Whether many practicing attorneys should be producing off-Broadway instead of doing what they're doing is a matter of conjecture which I must refuse to discuss here.

This book is being written from the point of view of the producer, and not from the point of view of the author. No slight of authors is intended, for I represent authors as well as producers. It's just that this book is about how to produce an off-Broadway play and not how to write an off-Broadway play. I couldn't begin to tell anyone how to write a play, for this I don't know myself. If I did know this, I would probably be writing plays instead of writing books on how to produce plays.

Hopefully, I can define for you certain concepts, ideas, and terms which are indefinable by normal expected standards. What I want to do is to discuss "specifics" in general. It will be impossible for me to pinpoint certain facts, but what I will have to do is to set broad limits within which your pinpoint may fall. In doing this, it is not my purpose in this book to explore the rare or unusual. There is enough divergence, that is, enough distance between the extremes on any given subject in off-Broadway contracts without finding the one in one thousand rarity which is way outside even those limits. The purpose of this book must be to define the usual outer limits within which most off-Broadway contracts and off-Broadway experience will fit, and at the same time to suggest what would be considered fair, reasonable or not unusual, bearing in mind what is right for one person may be all wrong for another.

Although you will notice my almost constant use of the words, "usually," "not unusual," "most of the time," "frequently," and similar words, parties entering into an agreement may agree to anything as long as they do not violate any law or agree to something contrary to public policy. If investors in a show consent that the general partner may use the funds to purchase a Rolls Royce for his own use in furtherance of the production, then he may do so. Anything is possible. Our discussion will confine itself to what is usual rather than to what is possible.

The problems which will be faced by an off-Broadway producer are in many ways similar to the problems of theatre producers throughout the country. The producer of a play for a university, community, or summer stock, will have to obtain the rights to do the play, will have to make arrangements with the investors, may have to satisfy the Securities and Exchange Commission, and most of the other things that are outlined in detail in this book with reference to off-Broadway producing. The minor details may be slightly different, but the basic concepts are the same.

1 Optioning a Property

The first thing that you must do as the producer of a play is to obtain a "property." "Property" is the word that is used to describe the play or other work which you want to perform or have performed. The author or owner of the play will either represent himself or be represented by an agent or by an attorney. When we refer to an owner, we may be referring to someone other than the author who may own the right to deal in the play, having inherited it or having purchased it. Unless otherwise specifically noted, all of the observations which refer to the author would be equally applicable to an owner of the play who is not the author.

On many occasions, I have been confronted by a client who has consulted me after he has just signed a piece of paper which he labels as an "option to produce an off-Broadway play." The client means well; he knows he needs legal advice and he's seeking it. Upon reading the "option," it becomes apparent that the client should have consulted an attorney before entering into this option agreement. The option agreement contains no provision for subsidiary rights (these will be explained in detail later) nor does it make provision for a right to tour the show or to do an English production of the show, if it is later deemed advisable. An option agreement that does not get for the producer everything that he ought to have is not just bad for the producer personally, but is also bad for the investors, and this could make it very difficult for the producer to raise the money to produce the play.

The producer consults his attorney, who will communicate with the author or the author's representative to discuss the various terms of the option. An option agreement is simply a grant of the rights to produce a play, in exchange for a money payment to the author. The amount of money paid, the length of the option, what the money payment buys, are all variables, negotiable items, which will be defined precisely in the option agreement.

Warranties and Representations

As the producer, you will want to make certain that the option to produce a play contains certain warranties and representations by the author or owner. In plain non-legal language this means simply that the author guarantees you, assures you, even insures you, that what he is selling to you is owned by him. He states in the agreement that he is either the author of the play or has acquired the rights to sell the play; that there have been no lawsuits that would endanger his ownership of the play, and that if it turns out that he does not own the play and you are damaged as a result, he will reimburse you to the extent that you have suffered from his misrepresentations. The warranties clause of an option agreement usually makes reference to the copyright ownership by the author or owner, and states the date and number of the copyright registration.

Length of the Option

Off-Broadway options can run for various terms; however, it is not unusual to have an option for a six-month period which can be extended for an additional six months upon payment of an additional sum of money. It then may be extended for an additional six months after that for still an additional sum of money. A six months option means that the play must open before a paying audience on or before six months from the date of the option agreement. Sometimes an option will be for a one year period with the right to extend the option for an additional six months or one year. One should bear in mind when negotiating the option that off-Broadway shows almost never open during the summer months; in fact, it is considered bad business to open an off-Broadway show after the month of April. With this thought in mind, in negotiating the option it is sometimes possible to convince the author or the author's representative, that for payment of the same amount of money that is requested for a six month option, the author really should grant a nine month option. This argument could be advanced especially if you are negotiating the option to become effective the early part of March. It is obvious that if you take an option in March with all the other work that has to be done, it will be next to impossible to produce the play to open before the end of April. From March 1st through August 31st would be six months, during two of which months it would be impossible to open and four of these months are months that are considered as not desirable opening dates. Under such circumstances one might convince the author to grant the option for a period of nine months, that is, until the end of November, for the same amount of money requested for a six month option, since the producer under such circumstances would just be buying the right to produce the play to open during the three months of September, October, and November.

Option Cost

In exchange for the right to produce the play to open on or before a specific date, a producer pays a sum of money which is usually considered to be an advance against royalties. The term, "advance against royalties" means exactly what it sounds like. This payment, being an advance against royalties, means that the amount of the payment is deducted from the first royalties earned by the author.

The amount of the option payment is not always the same, as this amount is determined by a number of factors. A well-known playwright who has many Broadway productions to his credit will of course demand and receive a larger option payment than an unknown author who has never had a play produced. In all events, the author's motivation, how badly he wants to see the play produced, the rapport between the producer and the author, the existence of other producers who may be anxious to produce the play, and such other similar factors, can influence the amount of money that will be demanded and paid for the option. A six month option may cost between $100 and $750. Payments usually range in the neighborhood of $250 to $350 for a six month option, and an additional $150 to $350 for extending the option another six months. A one year option usually costs in the area of $500 to $750 with a provision that the option may be extended for six months upon the payment of an additional $250 to $350.

I almost always negotiate on behalf of my producer clients with the thought in mind that it is far preferable to pay more money for the second six months of the option period than one pays for the first six months of the option period. The theory is that after a producer has owned the option for a period of six months, he should be in a pretty good position to know whether or not he will be able to raise the money, obtain a director, cast the play, and get it on. If things look good at the end of six months, then the additional larger payment is money well spent, as it is being spent for something which will be used, namely the right to produce the play. Furthermore, the additional payment is, like the first payment, an advance against royalties, and will be deducted from the first royalty payments in all events. If, after owning the option for six months, the producer decides that it is unlikely that he will be able to get the play produced, having paid less for the first six months he has saved some money which he will surely be able to use for the purchase of another property.

Play Cost (Royalties)

The payment previously referred to as an option payment is a payment for the right to produce the play. As soon as the play is presented before paying audiences, the producer makes a weekly payment to the author or owner which is a payment for the presentation of the play. The amount of the payment is directly related to the gross receipts of the producer from the sale of tickets. If the play is a non-musical, and the author is not a famous or well-known author or personality, the author is almost always paid five (5%) percent of the gross weekly box-office receipts. If the play is a musical and the author, composer, and lyricist are not well-known personalities or famous, the royalty payment is almost always six (6%) percent of the gross weekly box-office receipts. The author, composer, and lyricist, will either share the six (6%) percent of the gross weekly box-office receipts with the composer receiving two (2%) percent, the lyricist receiving two (2%) percent and the bookwriter receiving two (2%) percent, or they will share the six (6%) percent with the composer and lyricist together receiving three (3%) percent and the bookwriter receiving three (3%) percent of the gross weekly box-office receipts. The method of sharing is not really the producer's worry or responsibility, except to the extent that the producer must make the payment to specific parties in accordance with the agreement.

If the author (composer or lyricist if it be a musical) is a famous or well-known person, then the royalty payment may be, but need not always be, as much as ten (10%) percent of the gross weekly box-office receipts. I have noticed on numerous occasions that some well-known writers have insisted on restricting the royalty payments to them in an amount that would be paid to an unknown author, knowing that there are limitations to what an off-Broadway production ought to pay for a play, and that it is healthy for the play if the royalty payments are not excessive.

When we speak of the gross weekly box-office receipts, it must be understood that these receipts are almost always defined to be the gross receipts at the box-office from the sale of tickets, less theatre party commissions, discount and cut-rate sales, all admissions taxes present or to be levied, any union pension and welfare deductions, any subscription fees and actor's fund benefits.

Before leaving the subject of royalty payments, it is wise to be aware of a useful method of resolving a royalty disagreement which will be helpful in some instances. It may be suggested that the royalty payments should be increased after the production has recouped its original pre-production and production budget; that is, after the total amount of the investment has been recovered. If there is, for an example, a deadlock with the author insisting upon receiving six (6%) percent of the gross weekly box-office receipts, and the producer being inclined to pay no more than five (5%) percent of the gross weekly box-office receipts, it might be helpful to compromise with an arrangement which provides that the author is to be paid five (5%) percent of the gross weekly box-office receipts until the investors have recouped their original investment, at which time the author's royalty payments will be increased to six (6%) percent of the gross weekly box-office receipts. This is typical of one of the many compromises that may be made which help resolve disputes and bring about an agreement which might otherwise be difficult or impossible.

What the Option Buys

An option agreement must somewhere within it state that in consideration of the producer's payment of a certain amount of money, the producer has the right to produce the play to open off-Broadway on or before a specific date which is set forth in the option agreement.

What an Option Conditionally Buys

right to tour

In addition to the right to produce the play off-Broadway, the producer, under most circumstances, also ought to acquire the rights to produce the play in other areas conditioned upon the off-Broadway production running for a certain length of time. For an example, it is not unusual for the producer to acquire the rights to do a tour of the play in the event that the play opens and runs off-Broadway for twenty-one (21) performances. Bear in mind that under some circumstances this right may be acquired by running less than 21 performances or under other circumstances by running more than 21 performances. Also be cognizant of the fact that the number of performances for the purpose of this computation is defined in several ways.

Sometimes the contract provides that the play must run for 21 performances counting from the first paid performance, which would, of course, mean from the first paid preview. Other contracts provide that the show must run for 21 performances counting from opening night. When there is a disagreement on this item, a compromise is sometimes reached which would permit one to count 21 paid performances from the first paid preview; however, the number of paid previews would be limited to seven, ten, or at the most fourteen previews. Otherwise, it would be possible to acquire the rights to do a tour by running 21 paid previews and not opening the show. Bear in mind also that this method of computing the number of performances that the production has run will be important to us in our later discussion of subsidiary rights. We will see that a producer may acquire an interest in the subsidiary rights providing that the production runs for a certain number of performances.

The option agreement should, of course, set forth the fact that if the producer wishes to do a tour, either a first-class tour or a second-class tour, then the producer must within a certain period of time, for example, up to 90 days after the close of the play, or within one year of the opening of the play, give notice to the author of his intention to do the additional production. The option agreement will further provide that together with the notice the producer must make an advance payment against royalties, which advance payment will range between $150 and $500. Although there is no usual payment, $250 or $300 is more usual than either $150 or $500. The option must also provide that the tour must open within a specified time after the notice is received, and it is not unusual to provide that the period is one year after receipt of the notice within which the first performance on the tour must commence.

The Dramatists Guild, Inc. Minimum Basic Production Contract specifies terms for a first-class tour and refers to a second-class tour, but does not define the terms. Although it is difficult to define the term first-class tour other than as the Dramatists Guild, Inc. Contract has defined it, namely a regular evening bill in a first-class theatre in a first-class manner with a first-class cast and a first-class director, as a practical matter the distinction between first-class and second-class can usually be made without too much difficulty. We know that a Broadway production is a first-class production, and if the New York company of the show goes on tour it will appear in houses considered as first-class theatres and will be a first-class tour. An unusually successful Broadway show may have two or three first-class tours at the same time. There may also be a second-class tour of the same play. The author's royalties for a second-class tour of a Broadway show are usually calculated on a guarantee or flat fee basis; the author's royalties for a first-class tour are calculated on a percentage of the gross weekly box-office receipts.

Certain theatres have established themselves as first-class theatres because of the kind of productions which have appeared there. For example, the Mechanic in Baltimore; the Fisher in Detroit; the O'Keefe and Royal Alexandra in Toronto; the Colonial, Shubert and Wilbur in Boston; the Shubert, Forrest, Locust, Erlanger and Walnut in Philadelphia; the Blackstone, McVickers, Shubert, and Studebaker in Chicago; the Shubert in Cincinnati; the Hartford and Music Center in Los Angeles; the Curran and Geary in San Francisco; the National in Washington, D.C.; the Clowes in Indianapolis; the Music Hall in Kansas City; the Hanna in Cleveland; the American in St. Louis; the Shubert in New Haven, Conn.; are some of the first-class theatres throughout the country.

In addition to a second-class tour paying the author's royalties on a guarantee or flat fee basis, the other things that tend to identify a second-class tour are the length of time that the show is presented for each stop. Second-class tours are usually one night stands or split weeks. What is commonly referred to as a "bus and truck tour" is almost always a second-class tour which plays the one night stands and split weeks, as is a university or college tour.

Although the subject matter seems to be confusing in theory, in practice most people in the business have a working knowledge of what the words mean.

In the event that the producer wishes to do a first-class tour, the option agreement will provide that the parties agree to enter into

a Dramatists Guild, Inc. Minimum Basic Production Contract covering such a tour within a short period after receipt of the notice given
by the producer that he wishes to produce a tour. All royalty payments to the author will be as provided in the said Dramatists Guild,
Inc. Minimum Basic Production Contract.
For an example:

1. If the tour is for a non-musical play, the author will be paid
five (5%) percent of the first $5000 of the gross weekly box-office
receipts plus seven and one-half (7½) percent of the next $2000 of
such receipts plus ten (10%) percent of all receipts in excess of
$7000. If payment would result in there being no operating profits
for a particular week, the author will be paid for that week an amount
which will not result in an operating loss, except in no week will the
author receive less than $250.

2. If the tour is for a musical play, the author will be paid a
weekly royalty in the amount of six (6%) percent of the gross
weekly box-office receipts. If payment would result in there being
no operating profits for a particular week, the author will be paid
for that week an amount which will not result in an operating loss,
except in no week will the author receive less than $500.

In the event that the tour is a second-class tour of an off-Broadway
show, it is not unusual to provide for a royalty payment of five percent of the gross weekly box-office receipts or 5% of the flat fee
payable to the off-Broadway producer.

english production

If the play runs for 21 performances, more or less depending
upon the negotiations (counting the 21 performances as above discussed) it is also not unusual for the producer to acquire the rights
to do an English production of the play. As with the tour provisions,
the option agreement will provide that under such circumstances the
producer must within a certain period of time, that is up to 90 days
of the close of the play or within one year of the opening of the
play, give notice to the author of his intention to do the English production. With the notice the agreement will provide that the producer

must make an advance payment against royalties which will range between $250 and $600. Three hundred and fifty or five hundred dollars is most usual for this advance payment for the rights to do an English production. It is also most usual to provide that the English production must commence within a period between six months and one year after the receipt of the notice.

The agreement may provide that the royalty payment for a West End London production is as provided in the Dramatists Guild, Inc. Minimum Basic Production Contract for such a production; that is, five (5%) percent of the first 750 pounds sterling of gross weekly box-office receipts, plus seven and one-half (7½%) percent of the next 500 pounds sterling of gross weekly box-office receipts, plus ten (10%) percent of the excess over 1250 pounds sterling of gross weekly box-office receipts for a non-musical, and six (6%) percent of the gross weekly box-office receipts for a musical.

A West End production in London is comparable to a Broadway production in this country. There is one significant difference however, and that is that a West End London production may be mounted for approximately one-third of the amount of money which would be required for the same show if produced on Broadway. If the production is other than in the West End of London, then it is not unusual to provide for a straight five (5%) percent of the gross weekly box-office receipts as a royalty payment.

right to move to broadway

The agreement may also further provide that the producer in addition to the other rights, has the right to initially open the play on Broadway, or to move the play from an off-Broadway theatre to a Broadway theatre. The agreement will provide that the producer must, immediately upon the decision to open the play on Broadway, or to move the play from an off-Broadway theatre to a Broadway theatre, enter into a Dramatists Guild, Inc. Minimum Basic Production Contract, which contract sets forth all of the terms and conditions of the agreement with the author concerning the Broadway production. The Dramatists Guild, Inc. Minimum Basic Production Contract is too detailed and involved to consider at this particular time, and since it is not applicable to an off-Broadway production, suffice it to say that the royalty payments for a straight dramatic production on Broadway are a minimum of five (5%) percent of the first $5000 of gross weekly box-office receipts, and seven and one-half (7½%) percent of the next $2000 of such receipts, and ten (10%) percent of all such receipts in excess of $7000. These are minimum requirements, and there are certain limitations such as out-of-town tryouts. For a Broadway musical the minimum payment is six (6%) percent of the gross weekly box-office receipts as a royalty. It will be noted that these royalty payments are the same as are provided for a first-class tour, it being understood that a Broadway production is a first-class production in the same fashion that a tour of first-class theatres constitutes a first-class production.

subsidiary rights

Few subjects in connection with off-Broadway productions cause as much confusion as surrounds the area of "subsidiary rights." Many persons in theatre toss the term around knowing that they're supposed to know something about "subsidiaries," but not being sure just exactly what it is they're supposed to know or what they are supposed to do about it.

Subsidiary rights are rights which accrue to the producer as a result of his original production of the play. The right to produce the play in other places and in other media, such as the right to do a tour or to produce a movie, is a subsidiary right. Confusion arises because most often when people speak of "subsidiaries" or "subsidiary rights" they are not referring to the rights to produce the play in other areas or in other media, but rather they are referring to the producer's right to share in the author's receipts from productions of the play in other areas and in other media.

There is no doubt that when a play is produced off-Broadway (or on Broadway for that matter), that the production makes a contribution to the value of uses of the play in other media. The author may receive great revenue from the leasing rights, that is the rights which are granted to theatre groups throughout the country, both amateur and professional, to perform the play, not to mention the fact that the movie and television value of a property is enhanced by a successful off-Broadway production. The standard Dramatists Guild, Inc. Minimum Basic Production Contract (applicable of course to a Broadway production or other first-class production) provides that after 21 consecutive performances in New York the producer will be entitled to receive forty (40%) of the author's receipts from the subsidiaries therein named. There are other provisions in the Dramatists Guild, Inc. Contract providing that the interest in the subsidiary rights may be acquired if the show runs for 64 consecutive performances either in New York or out of New York, providing that said 64 performances shall have been given within 80 days of the first performance, and a provision that if the author consents and the producer has made a certain payment in accordance with the contract, the interest in the subsidiary rights may be acquired in one performance in New York. However, most author's will not consent to this latter alternative being part of the contract as finally signed. There is a wide variance in the off-Broadway contract provisions dealing with the producer's acquisition of an interest in the subsidiary rights.

Bear in mind that the author alone retains the right to deal with the property. The author will make the arrangements for, and will execute the contract if there is a sale for a movie or television production, or for any other use, and the producing company's interest is only in the sharing of the profits and not in the consummation of the actual sale. There is an exception in the case of the original cast album for a musical production in that the producing company, as well as the author, composer, and lyricist, will negotiate and enter into this agreement. However, the producer's being part of this agreement is not because of any interest in the subsidiary rights but rather because the original cast album will be made using the original cast of the show and the original cast is employed by the producer. It is, in effect, more than just a recording of the music, but is in a sense a recording of the production, or rather a part of the production.

Of course the author must deal in good faith with the property, which the author would normally do for the author's own sake as well as for the producing company's sake. He may not make a deal in which he sacrifices one of the properties that he has written, so that he may make a much better deal on another property which he has written, for such an arrangement would constitute an unfair dealing with respect to the first property.

For an example: an author may have a play that a movie producer is most anxious to make into a movie, for which the author has been offered $100,000. In the event that a producing company which produced the play has an interest in the subsidiary rights, then the author may not offer the right to do the movie for $75,000 on the condition that the movie producer will at the same time purchase another of his works for $50,000.

The subsidiary rights in which the producer acquires an interest, as set forth in the Dramatists Guild, Inc. Minimum Basic Production Contract, consist of motion picture (throughout the world) and the following with respect to the continental United States and Canada: radio; television; second-class touring performances; foreign language performances; condensed and tabloid versions; so-called concert tour versions; commercial uses; play albums of records, and under certain circumstances, stock performances and amateur performances. The Dramatists Guild, Inc. Minimum Basic Production Contract for a dramatico-musical production includes in addition to the above, grand opera in the United States and Canada. An off-Broadway option will usually include all of the above-listed subsidiaries in which the producer may acquire an interest, and may also include the receipts from a first-class tour, a Broadway production, or other off-Broadway productions. The off-Broadway option agreement will sometimes provide that the producer will acquire an interest in all of the subsidiary rights mentioned throughout the world without limiting them to the continental United States and Canada.

If the play runs for the length of time we referred to in the Dramatists Guild, Inc. Minimum Basic Production Contract, then a Broadway production would receive forty (40%) percent of the net receipts from the disposition of any of the subsidiaries listed, for a period of ten years after the last performance of the first- class run of the play; would receive 35% of the net receipts for the next succeeding two years; 30% for the next succeeding two years; 25% for the next succeeding two years; and 20% for the next succeeding two years after that, at which time the producer's interest in the receipts from said subsidiaries would cease. One should note that the producer will receive this percentage if the rights are disposed of during the time set forth, even if the payment is actually received after this time. For an example, if there is a movie sale made within ten years after the last performance of the first-class run of the play, then the producer would receive 40% of the net receipts from this movie sale, even though the payment may be received long after the expiration of the ten year period.

In an off-Broadway option agreement, the producer may acquire a percentage interest in the author's receipts from subsidiary rights that is either greater or less than what is provided in the Dramatists Guild, Inc. Minimum Basic Production Contract for a Broadway show. The extremes are: (1) the producer may acquire no interest in the subsidiary rights or (2) the producer may acquire 40% (or more than 40%) upon the first paid performance. Since the first paid performance could be the first paid preview, it is possible in such an extreme instance to acquire an interest in the subsidiary rights without ever opening the play. This has happened but is a rarity and is not the usual situation by any means.

A refusal to grant any interest in the subsidiary rights comes most often from foreign authors, although they are gradually changing this arbitrary position and are becoming educated to the facts of off-Broadway life. Even a famous foreign author makes it very difficult, if not impossible, for his producer to raise the money to produce the show if the producing company will end up with no interest in the subsidiary rights.

You may perhaps wish to produce a play which has been produced before, either on Broadway, in Europe, or elsewhere, and you may be confronted with an author who says: "I can't give you an interest in the subsidiary rights as I've already given away an interest to the producer who previously produced the show." There is a way to approach this problem that is sometimes helpful. Your response must be that the producer who produced the show originally ought to want to give some part of the subsidiary rights to the off-Broadway production, if the off-Broadway production runs for a certain length of time. There is good reason why the original producer would want

to do this in view of the fact that a successful off-Broadway production would increase the value of the subsidiary rights for all concerned, not only for the author but also for the original producer. It
may also be helpful to suggest that under such circumstances, in
addition to the original producer parting with some interest which
he owns in the subsidiary rights, that the author ought to grant the
off-Broadway producer some part of his remaining interest in said
subsidiary rights. If the original production owns a 40% interest
in the author's receipts from subsidiary rights, and you can convince
the original producer to part with 20% of the author's receipts, that
is half of the original producer's interest, you should be able to convince the author that he should give another 10%, which would
mean that the off-Broadway show could potentially receive 30%
of the receipts from the author's share of the subsidiary rights. The
original production would receive 20%, and the author would still
be left with 50%. The author in effect is getting two bites at the same
apple, and under such circumstances should not complain too much
about giving up an additional 10% interest and receiving something
slightly less. At the same time the original producer may discover
that the interest in the subsidiary rights is in effect found money,
so that he should not complain too much about having to give up
some of his share. The off-Broadway production will receive something slightly less, but this is a small price that one has to pay if one
wants to produce a show which has already been produced.

The off-Broadway option must make provision for the period of
time within which the sale must be made for the producer to share
in the profits from the subsidiary rights, and must make provision
for the amount of the profits which the producer will receive. In the
case of the length of time, the extremes in this instance are (1) three
years and (2) the life of the copyright plus the copyright renewal
which in this instance would be 56 years. What has become most
usual is that the interest of the off-Broadway producer will be paid
if any of the rights are disposed of during a period of 7 years, 10
years, or 18 years after the close of the off-Broadway play. Perhaps
the most commonly used period is 10 years for a dramatic play, and
either 10 or 18 years for a musical play.

Between the extreme of no interest in the subsidiary rights and the extreme of granting a 40% (or larger) interest upon the first paid performance, is the area where most contract negotiations end up. In an attempt to express the concept that the value that an off-Broadway production contributes to the property is directly proportionate to the length of time that the play runs off-Broadway, there has developed the idea of graduating the producer's share of the author's receipts so that the longer the play runs, the more the off-Broadway producer would receive from subsidiary rights. The producer's share is generally graduated between 10% of the receipts and 40% of the receipts. It is not unusual to grant the off-Broadway production 10% of the author's receipts if the play runs for 21 performances; 20% if the play runs for 42 performances; 30% if the play runs for 55 performances; and 40% if the play runs for over 68 performances. Bear in mind that I was careful to omit the time from which we start counting the 21 performances, 42 performances, or whatever number of performances. Although I omitted a reference to the starting time, you will remember our discussion in connection with the producer's acquisition of the rights to tour the play or to do an English production, and the discussion as to whether one counts the 21 performances from the first paid preview, from opening night, or from the first paid preview with a limitation on the number of previews that are counted. Although I was careful to omit the reference here, the negotiations which take place must settle this, and the option agreement which is drafted must carefully and explicitly set forth the time that one starts counting the performances.

Author's representatives will endeavor to sell you on the idea that you should accept 10% of the author's receipts if the play runs for 21 performances from opening night; 20% if the play runs for 56 performances from opening night; 30% if the play runs for 75 performances from opening night; and 40% if the play runs for 99 performances or over counting from opening night. The producer's attorney will, on the other hand, sell the author's representative on the idea that the producer should receive 10% of the author's share if the play runs for 21 paid performances; should receive 20% if the play runs for 35 paid performances; should receive 30% if the play runs for 48 paid performances; and should receive 40% if the play runs for 56 performances or more counting from the first paid performance.

Of course, it goes without saying that whether one counts from the first paid preview or from opening night, whether the interest of the off-Broadway producer in the subsidiary rights extends over a period of three years from the close of the off-Broadway production or 56 years from the close of the off-Broadway production, and the extent of the producer's interest in the rights, will depend upon the relative bargaining power of each of the parties.

Billing Credits

Another important provision in all option agreements is the provision concerning billing credits for the author. It is an especially important provision in the off-Broadway agreement since it very often provides the most meaningful consideration which the author receives. I have often said, partly in jest, that in negotiating an option agreement, the real quarrels do not concern money but rather the size of the type and whose name comes first. It's not only a matter of ego in a business where the amount of money one receives and one's importance in the profession is measured by the number of times that one's name is seen as well as the size of one's name. In a sense the argument about billing is in argument about money. Some of the stories concerning billing border upon the absurd; however, in the off-Broadway arena where the authors are paid relatively little, the authors' right to make their names known must be considered extremely important.

Some contracts provide that the author's name must appear in paid advertising, houseboards, billboards and programs. Teaser ads and alphabetical listing ads, commonly known as ABC ads, are usually the exception where the name need not appear. The newspapers, in fact, will not accept ABC ads for an off-Broadway show; however, this exclusion is always part of the clause pertaining to billing credits in the option agreement. Resist the author's attempt to have his name appear wherever the name of the play appears as there is no room on most marques for an author's name.

Sometimes there is a provision that the author's name will be a certain size in relation to the size of the type used for the title of the play; sometimes it is provided that the author's name will be at least one-half the size type used for the title of the play; or one-quarter of the size type used for the title of the play. Sometimes an author insists on a provision that his name will be as large or larger than any other name that appears in the advertisement, program or whatever. This may be a self-defeating provision as the producer may be placed in a position where he cannot sign a star or prominent director because he cannot give that star or prominent director the kind of billing that he insists upon in order to do the play. If the star insists that his name be larger than any other name, then it may very well be to the author's best interests to have the star's name larger than his. A producer must have the leeway to function so that the best artistic performers may be engaged for the play.

If there is more than one author, it is most usual that the authors' names appear in alphabetical order, unless one of the authors is much better known and thus in a position to insist that his name be first under all circumstances. I've known many writers to make no provision in a contract for their billing credits, because in their particular case this is not necessary. Many name writers know that the prominent use of their name by the producer will mean ticket sales for the producer. Ironically enough, the persons who are often in a sense in the best position to insist upon the most desirable billing credits often insist on nothing, knowing that they will receive the most desirable billing credits because it is in the interest of the producer to do this.

House Seats

An option agreement will almost always contain a provision providing that the author may purchase a certain number of house seats. House seats are prime seats which are reserved for purchase by various persons associated with the production, and are usually held by the theatre for the party until 6:00 P.M. of the day before each evening performance and until 12:00 noon of the day before each matinee performance. If the tickets are not purchased by then by the house seat owner, they are sold to the general public. It is usual for a producer to reserve one or two pairs of house seats for purchase by the author (more or less depending upon the size of the theatre) and five or six pairs for opening night.

Authors' Approvals

An option agreement will provide that the author shall have director approval, cast approval, and sometimes stage manager, costume designer, and set designer approval. In the case of a musical the composer may have musical director and choreographer approval. It should always further provide that the approvals will not be unreasonably withheld, and that if the author does not approve or disapprove within a certain specified time, that is within three to seven days after the request for approval, that the failure to respond shall be deemed to be an approval. The author may be out of the country or otherwise inaccessible, and the play must never suffer as a result of any one person's unavailability or disinterest.

It goes without saying that the agreement should provide that no changes will be made in the script without the author's approval. Rest assured that the author or the author's representative will make certain that this provision is part of the agreement. The producer might also insist that this approval by the author will also not be unreasonably withheld.

Arbitration

Options very often contain an arbitration clause which provides that if there is a dispute, instead of going to court to settle it, the parties consent that it may be settled by an impartial arbitrator, usually in accordance with the rules of the American Arbitration Association. The advantages of an arbitration are that it is informal, speedy, less expensive, and there is a clear probability that the dispute will be settled by a person or persons who know the business. Since the parties have an opportunity to select the arbitrators, the selection should be from a group of individuals involved in show business so that the party making the determination will have the background necessary to properly decide the issues.

Assignability of Option

The producer is given the right to assign the option agreement; however, this is usually granted with some limitations. An assignment is in effect a transfer. If one assigns a contract, the person taking the assignment, that is the person acquiring the rights to the contract, will receive all of the benefits of the contract, but at the same time assumes all of the contract obligations. The agreement may limit the assignment to only a limited partnership or corporation or other entity in which the producer is one of the major principals. The author originally makes his agreement with a specific producer, and does not want someone else producing the play, thus the provision that the entity must have as one of the principals the producer to whom the grant was originally made. An assignment is made subject to the terms and conditions of the original option agreement, which means that the company that is going to produce the show to which the producer makes the assignment, must be bound by the agreement. It is often provided that even if there is an assignment, the producer will continue to remain responsible for the obligations of the contract.

Option of First Refusal

The option may also contain a provision that the producer, if he successfully produces the play, may have an option of first refusal on future plays of the author. This means simply that the producer may match any other bonafide offer for the play during a fixed period of time and obtain the rights to produce the play under the same terms and conditions as the bonafide offer. An "option of first refusal" is a common term used in the business and this is its meaning; namely that the person holding the option during this given time must first be given an opportunity to make the purchase or do whatever is required before a sale may be made to someone else. There is much criticism of this kind of a provision since it is argued, and with good reason, that if the producer produces the play and he gets along well with the author, there is every reason in the world for the author to make certain that this producer produces his next play. If they do not get along, the producer should not produce the next play no matter what the contractual arrangements may be.

Buyers' Market

In the option negotiations it is well to bear in mind that off-Broadway is a buyers' market, in that an author who has never had a play produced often needs an off-Broadway production as a stepping stone to other writing assignments. There is this to be said however, that I do not, in all my experience, know of a really good play which has not been produced. I do know of really good plays that have been badly produced. However, if one has authored a play that has commercial and artistic possibilities, there is every reason to believe that this play will eventually be produced, "buyers' market" or not.

Typical Option

The following is a typical option agreement which might be applicable to an off-Broadway musical. Please bear in mind that this is not an average agreement as there is no such thing as an average agreement. It should be obvious by now that rarely are there two option agreements with the same terms throughout the entire agreements.

AGREEMENT made as of this 1st day of March, 1968 between Daniel Doe and Richard Roe, (sometimes hereinafter referred to as the "Producer") and Jimmy Jones and Sally Smith, (the Bookwriter-Lyricist and Composer), (sometimes hereinafter jointly referred to as the "Authors" or the "Owners"), with respect to the option to perform the musical play presently entitled, "Fiction" (sometimes hereinafter referred to as the "Play").

1. The Owners do hereby warrant and represent that they are the sole owners of the Play which Play was originally copyrighted under the name, "Fiction" under Registration Number DU 00000, dated April 24th, 1964, and the Authors are the Owners of the said copyright and they have the right to deal with all the rights herein granted. The Authors further warrant and represent that the Play does not infringe upon the copyright of any other work or violate any other rights of any other person, firm, corporation, or other entity, and that no claim has been made against the Owners, adversely affecting the Play or the copyright, or any of the rights herein granted, and the Owners have full power to enter into this Agreement and do hereby agree to indemnify and hold the Producer harmless against any claims, demands, suits, losses, costs, expenses, damages or recoveries, by reason of any violation of proprietary rights with respect to the Play or which the Producer may suffer as a result of the warranties and representations herein made, pursuant to this option.

2. The Owners do hereby grant to the Producer the sole and exclusive right and license to produce the Play and to present it as a professional off-Broadway production in an off-Broadway theatre

in the City of New York. In consideration of the sum of Five Hundred ($500) Dollars paid upon the signing of this contract, receipt of which is hereby acknowledged, the Owners do hereby grant to the Producer the option to produce the Play to open on or before February 28, 1969. The Producer may extend this option to open the Play on or before September 30, 1969, upon payment to the Authors of an additional Three Hundred and Fifty ($350) Dollars on or before February 28th, 1969. The payments hereinbefore provided shall be deemed to be non-returnable advances against the royalties hereinafter provided for.

3. The rights granted to the Producer are the sole and exclusive rights to produce the Play off-Broadway in New York City (Producer may acquire an option pursuant to the terms of this Agreement as hereinafter set forth to produce the play on tour or in the British Isles) and the Owners agree that they will not grant the rights nor permit anyone to perform the said Play in any medium within the United States of America, Canada or the British Isles, during the term of the option herein granted and the run of the Play or during the period that the Producer retains any rights or option to produce the Play anywhere in the United States, Canada or the British Isles, and further agree that they will not grant the right to anyone to do a movie version of the said Play which would be released during the term of the option or the run of the Play or during the period the Producer retains any rights or option to produce the Play in the United States, Canada or in the British Isles.

4. The Owners shall be paid six (6%) percent of the gross box-office receipts as a royalty payment during each week. The gross box-office receipts shall mean all receipts at the box-office from the sale of tickets less theatre party commissions, discount and cut-rate sales, all admission taxes presently or to be levied, any pension and welfare deductions, any subscription fees and actor's fund benefits. The Producer agrees to keep accurate books and records and will furnish the Owners a signed box-office statement, together with each royalty payment which will be made on or before each Wednesday for the previous week's performances, and the Owners or their representatives shall have the right to examine the books and records of the Producer pertaining to the Play, upon giving the Producer reasonable notice.

5. If the Play is produced within the option period, herein granted, the right to produce the Play off-Broadway shall continue during its continuous run.

6. Although the Producer is acquiring the rights and services of the Owners, solely in connection with the production of the Play, the Owners recognize that by a successful production, the Producer makes a contribution to the value of uses of the Play in other media. Therefore, although the relationship between the parties is limited to play production as herein provided, and the Owners alone own

and control the Play with respect to all other uses, nevertheless, if the Producer has produced the Play as provided herein, the Owners agree that the Producer shall receive the percentage of net receipts (regardless of when paid) specified herein below, if the Play has been produced for the number of consecutive performances (including paid preview performances if the Play opens off-Broadway, however, no more than 14 preview performances shall be used in this computation) specified below, and if, before the expiration of fifteen (15) years, subsequent to the date of the last public performance of the Play, off-Broadway, any of the following rights are disposed of anywhere throughout the world: motion picture; or with respect to the continental United States and Canada any of the following: radio; television; touring performances; stock performances; Broadway performances; off-Broadway performances; amateur performances; foreign language performances; condensed and tabloid versions; so-called concert tour versions; commercial uses; and play albums or records: Ten (10%) percent if the Play shall run for twenty-one (21) off-Broadway performances commencing with the first paid preview performance hereunder; twenty (20%) percent if the Play shall run for thirty-four (34) off-Broadway performances commencing with the first paid preview performance hereunder; thirty (30%) percent if the Play shall run for forty-four (44) off-Broadway performances commencing with the first paid preview performance hereunder; forty (40%) percent if the Play shall run for fifty-two (52) off-Broadway performances commencing with the first paid preview performance hereunder. For the purpose of computing the number of performances, providing the Play officially opens off-Broadway in New York City, the first paid performance shall be deemed to be the first performance, however, no more than fourteen (14) preview performances shall be used in making the computation.

7. For all public performances of the Play, the Producer shall make available for purchase by Jimmy Jones and Sally Smith or their designees, at regular box-office prices, to each of them one adjoining pair of orchestra tickets in the first six (6) center rows of the theatre. Such tickets shall be held at the box-office until 6:00 P.M. of the day before each evening performance and until 12:00 noon of the day before each matinee performance. Producer also agrees to make available for purchase by each of them or their designees, five (5) pairs of seats in a desirable location in the orchestra center for the official opening of the Play off-Broadway in New York City.

8. The Producer agrees to give the composer and bookwriter-lyricist credit in all advertisements except ABC ads or "teasers" in which only the name of the Play and the theatre appear, and will at all times give credit in all programs, billboards, houseboards, wherever the name of the Play appears. The composer's credits and the bookwriter-lyricist's credits will be of a type of the same size and prominence and their names will appear immediately under

the title in type at least one-half the size of the type used in the title. No name shall be in type larger than the type used for the composer and bookwriter-lyricist except for the name of a star performer, or a director of prominence.

9. In the event that the Play opens off-Broadway, then the Producer is granted the right up to ninety (90) days after the close of the off-Broadway production of the Play, to give notice that the Producer wishes to contract for the touring rights to the Play in the United States upon the following terms and conditions: If the tour is to be a first-class tour, then upon the terms and conditions as set forth in the Dramatists Guild Minimum Basic Production Contract for such a tour, including such advances or option payments as set forth therein as well as royalty terms covering such first-class tour, and the parties agree to sign a Dramatists Guild Minimum Basic Production Contract for such production; if the tour is to be a second-class touring company, the royalty to be paid shall be six (6%) percent of the gross box-office receipts (as herein defined). In the event that the Producer contracts to produce the Play upon payment to the Producer of a flat fee, such as a concert or college tour, then in such event the Owners shall be paid a royalty of six (6%) percent of the contracted fee. Upon receipt by the Owners of written notice from the Producer within ninety (90) days of the closing of the off-Broadway production, the parties agree to expeditiously thereafter enter into a contract containing the above terms, which contract shall provide for a payment to the Owners of a nonreturnable advance against royalties in the amount of Three Hundred and Fifty ($350) Dollars, and shall further provide that said tour, may commence at any time up to twelve (12) months of the closing of the off-Broadway production.

10. The Producer shall have the exclusive right during the term of this option or any extensions thereof, to originally produce the Play on Broadway in New York City or to transfer the production to a Broadway theatre within sixty (60) days after the close of the off-Broadway run of the Play and in the event that the Producer exercises this right, the parties agree to enter into a Dramatists Guild Minimum Basic Production Contract within seven (7) days after receipt by the Owners of the Producer's written intention to exercise this said right.

11. In the event that the Play opens off-Broadway in New York City, then the Producer is granted the right up to ninety (90) days after the close of the off-Broadway production of the Play, to give notice that the Producer wishes to contract for the rights to produce the Play in the British Isles. In the event that the Producer exercises the option to produce the Play in the British Isles, the Producer will give the Owners a written notice up to ninety (90) days after the close of the off-Broadway production, and the parties agree to expeditiously thereafter enter into a contract containing the terms hereinafter set forth which contract shall provide that the

English production may open at any time up to twelve (12) months after the close of the off-Broadway production.

Said contract shall provide that the royalty payments to the Owners for the British Production Rights shall be as follows: for a first-class performance of the Play in the West End of London a sum equal to (6%) percent of all gross weekly box-office receipts. In the event of a West End production, the Producer shall acquire the same interest in the British subsidiary rights depending upon the length of the West End run as hereinabove provided in Paragraph 6 of this agreement for the off-Broadway production.

For all performances of the Play presented outside of the West End of London, a sum equal to five (5%) percent of all gross weekly box-office receipts shall be payable as royalties.

Said British contract, whether for the West End or outside of the West End, shall also provide for payment to the Owners of an advance against royalties in the amount of Five Hundred ($500) Dollars.

12. Anything to the contrary in Paragraph "6" of this Agreement notwithstanding, in the event that an original cast album is made of the musical Play, then it is agreed that such a contract shall be jointly negotiated by the Producer and the Authors and any contract entered into for an original cast album must be signed by both the Producer and the Authors. All net proceeds received from such an original cast album shall be shared with the Authors receiving sixty (60%) percent and the Producer receiving forty (40%) percent.

13. In the event that the Authors designate a licensing agency to represent them in connection with the disposition of any of the subsidiary rights set forth in Paragraph "6" of this Agreement, then the Producer shall receive the same percentage of the said net receipts received from the licensing agency that the Producer would receive pursuant to Paragraph "6" of this Agreement if there were no licensing agency.

14. The Authors are to have director, cast, choreographer, musical director, costume designer and set designer approval, which approval will not be unreasonably withheld. In the event that the Authors do not approve or disapprove within two (2) days of the request for their approval, it shall be deemed to be an approval.

15. In the event that the Play is produced off-Broadway and runs for twenty-one (21) performances from the official opening, then the Producer shall be entitled to an option of first refusal for the motion picture production rights and the television production rights based on the Play. In the event that the Authors are desirous of making a sale of either the motion picture rights or the television rights, they must first give the Producer, under such circumstances, the opportunity to match any bonafide offer. The Authors must give

the Producer notice of any bonafide offer and within two weeks of the receipt of such offer, the Producer must enter into an Agreement with the Authors upon the same terms and conditions as the said bonafide offer, and if an Agreement is not entered into within the said two weeks, then the Authors are free to deal with the property and to sell it to a third party providing, however, that any such sale must be on terms no less desirable to the Authors than the terms as set forth in the notice to the Producer. Under all circumstances if the Producer acquires either the motion picture production rights or the television production rights pursuant to this Paragraph, then unless the motion picture or television production is actually completed (that is principal photography must have been completed or the television production must have been reduced to tape or actually have been shown live) within three (3) years of the date of the Agreement conveying the rights to the Producer, all such production rights shall revert to the Authors. In the event that the Producer produces either the motion picture or the television production, then, the Producer shall not be entitled to any interest in the subsidiary rights as set forth in Paragraph "6" of this Agreement for any production in which the Producer is actually directly or indirectly involved as the Producer. In the event that the motion picture and/or television production is produced by someone other than the Producer, then the Producer would be entitled to the percentage interest in said motion picture or television rights as is set forth in Paragraph "6" of this Agreement.

16. The Play shall be deemed closed (that is, the continuous run shall have terminated) if no paid performances have been given off-Broadway for a period of one (1) month. After the Play has closed and after all options to produce the Play have expired then the rights herein granted to produce the Play shall revert to the Owners, subject to any other terms specifically herein set forth.

17. Any controversy or claim, arising out of, or relating to this Agreement, or the breach thereof, shall be settled by arbitration in New York, N.Y., in accordance with the rules then obtaining of the American Arbitration Association and judgment upon the award rendered may be entered in any court of the forum having jurisdiction hereof.

18. This Agreement shall be binding upon and inure to the benefit of the parties, their respective heirs, next of kin, executors, administrators, successors, assigns, and legal representatives.

19. The Producer may assign this Agreement to a Limited Partnership or to a Corporation or other entity in which the Producer is one of the major principals; however, any assignments shall be subject to all of the terms and conditions of this Agreement and any assignee must agree to be bound by this Agreement.

20. This Agreement represents the entire understanding of

the parties and cannot be changed or amended unless by a document in writing, duly signed by the parties hereto.

21. All rights not specifically herein granted to the Producer are reserved for the Owners.

22. The Producer shall make no script or music changes without the respective Owners' approval, which approval will not be unreasonably withheld.

23. All notices herein provided for shall be sent by registered mail or by telegram to the parties as follows:
Daniel Doe, 886—33rd Avenue, New York, N.Y.; Richard Roe, 886—33rd Avenue, New York, N.Y.; Jimmy Jones, 21077 Park Avenue, New York. N.Y.; Sally Smith, 24—14th Avenue, New York, N. Y.; A copy of all notices will be sent to John A. Counselor, 46th Street and Park Avenue, New York, N.Y.

IN WITNESS WHEREOF the parties hereto have hereunto set their hands and seals as of the day and year first above written.

_____	_____
Daniel Doe	Richard Roe
_____	_____
Jimmy Jones	Sally Smith

Adaptations

No one in their right mind would go into the street, find an automobile which appeals to him, and start washing and polishing that automobile in the hope that when the owner returned to the car, he would purchase the automobile from him. Although no one would do this to an automobile, some people very often without thinking, do obtain a property which belongs to someone else, and go to great lengths to improve the property without first owning it. What I am referring to is the common practice of adapting a novel, a movie, or a non-musical as a musical for a stage production when the basic rights are not owned. Composers do it, writers do it, even producers do it. When one wishes to adapt or cause to be adapted a novel, story, movie, or whatever, which was written by someone else, one must first acquire the rights to make the adaptation.

basic work — copyright ownership

It is sometimes difficult to determine who is the owner of the "basic work" (as it is referred to) and the first thing that must be done is to obtain a copyright search. The copyright search should disclose whether or not the basic work is in the public domain, and if it is not in the public domain, who the copyright owner of record is. When we speak about "public domain," we of course mean that the work does not enjoy copyright protection, either because the copyright has expired, the work was published without filing with the copyright office, or for some other reason. Although there are strong movements to change the copyright laws, and especially the length of the copyright protection, at the present time the law provides that the original filing protects the work for a period of 28 years, and the renewal of the copyright extends the protection for an additional 28 years. When one sells a copyright, that is, assigns the copyright to someone else, a document should be recorded in the copyright office. The copyright search will disclose this document if it has been filed.

royalties for basic work

The negotiations then commence with the copyright owner to obtain the rights to do the adaptation. It is most usual to pay one or two percent of the gross weekly box-office receipts to the owner of the basic work. Furthermore, the owner of the basic work will want an interest in the subsidiaries, and will request and will usually get that proportionate part of any payment which his royalty bears to the aggregate royalties payable to all of the authors (including the payment to the owner of the basic work). This means that if a total of 6% is paid to all the authors (including the payment to the owner of the basic work), and the owner of the basic work is paid a royalty of one percent, then the owner of the basic work will share in the subsidiaries by receiving one-sixth of the author's share of said subsidiaries.

basic work option fee

It is not unusual for a producer to find a basic work which he wants adapted, and to cause the adaptation to be made. In addition to the provision for royalty payments, there are many other details of the agreement dealing with the acquisition of the rights to do an adaptation of the basic work. For an off-Broadway production it is not unusual to obtain these rights without the payment of a large sum of money as a fee, or as an advance against royalty payments. In some instances, it is possible to obtain these rights without any advance payment, although it is not unusual to pay the sum of $250 or $350 as an advance against royalty payments. This payment will purchase the right to do the adaptation which must be completed within a specified time, often within one year, and the right to produce the play within a specified time, usually a year after the completion of the adaptation.

the adapter

An off-Broadway producer will have to find a book-writer (and in the case of a musical, a composer and lyricist) to do the adaptation. Most writers would not begin to do a play for a producer for a Broadway production without a payment of money, the amount of money being dependent upon the reputation of the writer, and how badly the writer wants to do the play. Off-Broadway, it is not unusual to find writers who are willing to do an adaptation on "spec," which means that the work is done on the speculation that after it is completed, it will be sold. A full option agreement must be entered into with the person doing the adaptation, which agreement will provide that the producer may produce the play after it is completed. It usually further provides that the producer shall continue to own the basic rights, and if the producer is not happy with the adaptation, the rights in the basic work revert to the producer, who can at this point go out and hire another to do the adaptation of the work.

The important lesson that one should learn is that before we improve something, we should make certain that we own it, whether it be an automobile, a house, a novel, or a movie.

2   Co-Production Agreements

Either before or after you've optioned the property, you may decide that you wish to produce the play together with someone else. If this be the case, it is wise for you to have an agreement in the nature of a co-production agreement, which sets forth your duties and obligations to each other. Before the limited partnership or other entity which will produce the play comes into existence, you and your co-producer are operating as an entity, usually in the nature of a "joint venture." A joint venture is a kind of partnership, and the one most important fact that you must bear in mind is that like other partnerships you are responsible for all of the acts of your joint venturer in connection with the business of the joint venture.

Although the agreement between you may state that you will each be equally responsible for any expenditures or any losses, as far as creditors of the joint venture are concerned, each of you is responsible for the total amount of the commitment. That is, if one of two joint venturers (partners) obligates the joint venture (partnership) to the extent of $4000 for advertising, or for any other business expenditure, each of the two partners as between themselves may be responsible for $2000 of this obligation. The creditor, however, may look to either one for his $4000 and if one of the partners does not have any money, the creditor may collect the whole $4000 from the solvent member of the joint venture.

The joint venture agreement will state that the co-producers own a property which they wish to produce, that they are going to endeavor to raise the money for the production, and when the money is raised, they will be the general partners of a limited partnership which will be formed. This agreement will set forth the basic terms which will be incorporated into the limited partnership agreement. There will also be set forth the amount of the budget, the method of sharing profits and losses by each of the partners, whether or not the partners' profits are related to the amount of money that each producer raises, how the producer's fees are to be shared, how the cash office charge is shared, and so forth.

The co-producers may agree that they will share equally in the profits of the company irrespective of which partner is responsible for the raising of most of the money for the show. On the other hand, sometimes co-producers wish to relate the share of the profits more directly to the amount of money which each one raises. If one is going to relate the sharing of the profits to the amount of money that each co-producer raises, one ought also to relate the other important contributions to the production to the sharing of the profits. For an example, the partner who discovered the property could claim a larger percentage of the profits for this contribution; the party influencing the star could claim something extra for that; and so on. The next logical step is an attempt to balance all of the items that each of the co-producers contributes, and to relate the share of the profits to the relative importance of each contribution. So very often, when co-producers sit down and try to balance the contribution that each one makes to a production, they discover that the importance of each contribution is difficult to measure. As a result they end up sharing equally in the profits and losses, with all parties agreeing to contribute their best efforts to the production in all ways.

Front Money

Where the front money is coming from, and what will be given for the front money is another item which must be dealt with in the co-production agreement. "Front money" is money that is obtained for the purpose of paying all the expenses which must be paid prior to the money-raising in earnest, and prior to the receipt of the total capitalization and release of the investors' funds. It is necessary to pay for the option, to pay for printing of scripts, to make a payment to the attorney, a payment to the general manager, and to have money available for the presentation of backers' auditions. The front money which the producer may raise, if he doesn't use his own money, may be given on the condition that the producer assign a certain percentage interest of the producer's partnership profits to the person putting up the front money.

Front money is discussed here because it is often the reason for taking a co-producer. Sometimes the co-producer will contribute the front money in exchange for your contributing the property, or at least for your discovery of the property. Even if both co-producers are to equally furnish front money, the facts, in all events, must be set forth in the co-production agreement.

The joint venture agreement will also set forth how decisions are to be made and what happens if there is a deadlock, as it is very important that there be some quick resolution in the event that there is a disagreement. In the case of an artistic decision, two co-producers may provide that in the event of a dispute by them, the director will make the final determination. They may also provide that in the event of a business dispute, the question will be settled by the attorney, the accountant, or anyone else whose business judgment both producers would respect. Other possibilities exist for settling such disputes as various as one's imagination.

The agreement should also set forth who may sign checks and who may sign other obligations of the joint venture. The ever-prevailing question of credits must be dealt with in this agreement, that is, whose name comes first. It is usual to provide that wherever the name of one co-producer appears, the name of all co-producers will appear in type of the same size, prominence, and boldness. Billing credits are usually in alphabetical order in the absence of other more pressing considerations. An arbitration clause may be included which, as we know, means that in the event of a dispute, rather than going to court, an impartial person would make the determination.

The joint venture agreement should also set forth the personnel that the producers have agreed upon who will be employed by the show, namely, the attorney, the accountant, and the general manager, as well as any other personnel that there is agreement upon at this stage.

The joint venture will cease upon the organization of the limited partnership unless the parties abandon the play and decide to terminate it sooner.

This is what a typical Joint Venture Agreement looks like. Again the caution that this is not an average agreement, as there is no such thing.

AGREEMENT made as of this 1st day of April, 1968, between DANIEL DOE (sometimes hereinafter referred to as "Doe"), RICHARD ROE (sometimes hereinafter referred to as "Roe"), and HAROLD HOE (sometimes hereinafter referred to as "Hoe").

FIRST: The parties hereto do hereby form a Joint Venture to be conducted under the firm name of The Fictitious Joint Venture, (hereinafter sometimes referred to as the "Joint Venture"), for the purpose of producing and presenting in an off-Broadway theatre the play presently entitled "Fiction," written by Thomas Toe.

SECOND: The parties agree, as soon as possible, to form a limited partnership under the laws of the State of New York (hereinafter sometimes referred to as the "limited partnership") to produce the said play. The said limited partnership will be known as the "Fiction Company."

(a) The parties hereto will be the general partners of the limited partnership, and the parties contributing to the capital thereof will be the limited partners of the partnership.

(b) The capital of the limited partnership will be in an amount not less than $30,000.00, or such other amount as may mutually be agreed upon among the parties to this agreement.

(c) The limited partnership agreement shall be based on a theatrical limited partnership agreement for an off-Broadway production, as prepared by John A. Counselor, the Attorney for the Joint Venture and for the limited partnership.

(d) Each party agrees to use his best efforts to raise the capital of the limited partnership. In the event that the parties hereto cannot raise the complete capital necessary for the limited partnership, and it is necessary to pay someone money or a share of the general partners' profits, for the raising of any part of said capital, if the parties hereto are in complete agreement with respect to such an arrangement, then the amount so paid to said party shall be contributed equally by the parties hereto.

(e) The limited partners shall receive fifty (50%) percent of the net profits of the limited partnership, and the general partners shall receive the remaining fifty (50%) percent of the net profits. The net profits shall first be used to repay the limited partners to the extent of their investment in the limited partnership before the profits are shared with the general partners.

If any star(s) is entitled to receive any part of the net profits, the same shall be deemed to be an expense and deducted before computing the net profits to be divided between the general and limited partners.

(f) Regardless of the amount of capital raised or contributed by each party to this agreement, the net profits remaining in the general partnership shall be divided equally among them, that is, Doe, 33-1/3%, Roe, 33-1/3%, and Hoe, 33-1/3%.

(g) Any net losses of the limited partnership over and above the capital thereof shall be borne by the parties hereto in the same proportion as they share in the general partners' share of the profits, that is, equally.

(h) The parties agree to assign to the limited partnership, at their original cost, all rights in and to the option to produce the play which they have heretofore acquired, and any other agreements entered into for the purpose of producing the play.

(i) The producers' fee payable by the limited partnership shall be in the amount of $150 and shall be shared equally by the parties to this agreement. The cash office charge in the amount of $75 shall be paid to Richard Roe.

THIRD: All contracts and all checks on behalf of the Joint Venture, and on behalf of the limited partnership, may be signed by any one of the parties to this agreement.

FOURTH: Any and all obligations of any kind or nature for the Joint Venture or for the limited partnership shall be incurred only upon the consent of a majority, that is upon the consent of two out of three of them.

Any and all decisions by the producers whether business or artistic decisions shall be decided by any two of the three producers, with each of the producers having one vote, and the parties agree to be bound by a vote of the majority.

Anything to the contrary hereinbefore stated notwithstanding, on the question as to whether or not the show should remain open if there is the possibility that additional capital will have to be invested by the parties to this agreement, then the determination to run the show which might expose the parties to additional liability must be unanimous, that is, must be concurred in by all three parties to this agreement.

FIFTH: Wherever producers' credits are given, the credits shall be in alphabetical order. It is agreed that Harold Hoe, who will be the Director, will not be listed as a producer. All producers' names as producers shall be of equal size, prominence and boldness. The parties are entering into an agreement with Harold Hoe to direct the production. The agreement with Hoe provides that the name of the Director will appear wherever the name of the Author appears, and his name will appear in all paid advertising except ABC ads, shallow double ads, and teasers. The Director will receive billing credits in the same size, style and boldness of type as the Author. His name will not appear on the marquee or on billboards or posters if deemed inappropriate by Doe and Roe.

SIXTH: Each party shall devote as much time as is reasonably necessary for the production and presentation of the play; it being recognized and agreed that each party may be engaged in outside activities, whether or not of a competing nature, so long as he devotes sufficient time to the Joint Venture and to the limited partnership, and to the proper running of the business of producing and presenting the play.

SEVENTH: The Joint Venture shall terminate upon the happening of the first of the following:

(a) The formation of the limited partnership;

(b) Such date as the parties hereto may mutually agree upon;

(c) The withdrawal of any of the parties hereto.

EIGHTH: It is agreed that the pre-production money, that is the front money, shall be furnished equally by the three parties to this agreement.

All monies so advanced, as well as other expenditures on behalf of the Joint Venture by any party approved by the other parties, shall be repaid to the party immediately upon full capitalization of the limited partnership.

NINTH: It is agreed that the following parties will be engaged by the Joint Venture and the limited partnership in the following capacities:

(a) Ada Column as accountant;

(b) John A. Counselor as the attorney;

(c) Harold Hoe as Director;

(d) Frank Foe as General Manager.

The Joint Venture is simultaneously with the execution of this agreement entering into an agreement with Harold Hoe, hiring him as the Director of the play. The parties to this agreement do acknowledge that they know all of the terms and conditions of said agreement.

TENTH: Any and all disputes or differences, in connection with this agreement or the breach or the alleged breach thereof, shall be submitted to arbitration to be held in New York City, under the rules and regulations of the American Arbitration Association then obtaining, and each of the parties hereto agree to be bound by the determination of the majority of the arbitrators. Judgment on the award rendered may be entered in the highest court of the forum, state or federal, having jurisdiction.

IN WITNESS WHEREOF the parties have set their hands and seals as of the day and year first above written.

—————————————————

Daniel Doe

—————————————————

Richard Roe

—————————————————

Harold Hoe

Associate Producer — Money

We have previously discussed a co-production agreement in the nature of a joint venture, and something should be said at this point about arrangements with associate producers. A co-producer, in a sense, is a partner who may have an equal amount of say-so in the running of the business, both artistically and from a business point of view. An associate producer, on the other hand, usually spells one thing and that is "money." Most associate producers get billing credit as an associate producer for having furnished, usually through someone else's investment, a certain amount of money for the show. What else the associate producer gets, in addition to associate producer billing depends upon how badly the producer needs the amount of money that the associate producer can furnish. A part of the producer's profits yes, but it almost never includes any decision-making on the artistic or business level. A smart producer will take into consideration any suggestions made by an associate producer even though there is no obligation to accept the associate's advice.

It is not unusual for the producer to give an associate producer one percent of the profits of the producing company payable from the general partners' share for each three percent, four percent or five percent of the producing company purchased by an investment for which the associate producer is responsible. This must not be confused with front money. Front money, which we previously discussed, is something else; it is money that can be used prior to the capitalization and formation of the producing company. Front money is risk capital in that if the show is not produced, then the front money investor loses the money spent on the production and ends up with a tax loss. The person furnishing the front money will generally get something more like one percent of the profits of the producing company payable from the general partners' share for each one percent of the producing company that that particular amount of money would buy from the limited partners' share of the profits. It is not unusual to give a person who furnishes front money associate producer's billing credits as well as the percentage interest in the show.

3   The Producing Company

After having acquired the property, you must give consideration to the type of entity that will produce the play. When we talk about an "entity," we mean the producing company. Of course, you may produce the play yourself in your own name instead of using a different, separate entity, but then you will be the sole producer and must furnish all of the money. If you borrowed all the money or had all the money in the bank, you might do it in this fashion; however, a play is almost always financed by persons making investments in a producing company rather than making a loan to the producer or a producer furnishing all of the money himself. If investors are going to give you money, some agreement must be reached between you as the producer and your investors. The entity which will produce the play, that is, the producing company, will either be a partnership or a corporation. It is almost always a partnership—a special kind of partnership known as a "limited partnership."

Partnership or Corporation

limited liability

Why use a limited partnership to produce the play—why not a corporation? This is a very good question. We rule out a general partnership or a joint venture immediately because it does not give the investors the benefit of limited liability. Limited liability means simply that the investors, the limited partners, are only obligated to the extent of their investment (or in some instances, if there is an overcall provided for in the agreement, they are liable to the extent of an additional ten (10%) percent, fifteen (15%) percent, or twenty (20%) percent). The general partner, the producer in a limited partnership, runs the business and is personally responsible for all of the obligations of the partnership. If the production goes over the budget and more money is spent than is raised, this becomes the obligation of the general partner. This is not the obligation of the limited partners, assuming of course, that the limited partnership is properly organized strictly in accordance with the terms of the Partnership Laws of the State of New York.

We could also give our investors limited liability if we formed a corporation and made them corporate stockholders. In this fashion, the producers could be the officers and directors and the investors would not be liable beyond the original investment.

tax benefits

Although corporate stockholders enjoy limited liability in the same sense that limited partners do, there are certain tax advantages that the investors enjoy with a partnership that they would not have with a corporation. If the company loses money, that is, if the venture does not make enough money to return to the investors their total investment, the loss for income tax purposes is considered an ordinary loss which may be offset against ordinary income if a partnership is the producer. Each partner would consider his investment to the extent it is lost, as an ordinary loss.

If a corporation is the producing company and it loses money, the loss is in the nature of a capital loss. Each investor may offset the loss, first against capital gains, and the balance, if any, may then be offset up to $1,000 of ordinary income. Since most investors need a loss which can be offset against income more than they need a capital loss, the benefit to the investor of a partnership is considerable in this respect.

The other important consideration is that partnership income is taxed but once. If the producing company is a corporation and makes a profit, the corporation first pays income tax on the income and then when the profits are distributed to the investors as dividends, the investors again pay an income tax on the dividends.

Corporation As a Partner

The laws of the State of New York were changed effective September 1, 1963, to provide that a corporation may be a general partner or limited partner. You may ask why not combine the advantages of a corporation and the advantages of a partnership, that is, have the producer or producers first organize a corporation and make this corporation the general partner of the limited partnership, so that the investors may have the tax benefits of a partnership, and the producer as well as the investors may have the advantage of limited liability. There are some instances where this may be advisable. If the corporation is substantial and has large assets, then there may be good reason and less risk to do this. If, however, you organize a new corporation which has no assets and it is obviously being organized solely for the purpose of becoming a general partner of a limited partnership, then there is an unresolved question as to whether or not the Internal Revenue Service would consider the producing company to be a partnership or to be a corporation for income tax purposes. Eminent theatrical accountants inform me that to date there has not been a specific ruling that would further clarify the Internal Revenue Service's position on this issue.

There is still another alternative if one wishes a corporation to be a general partner, and if one of the producers is less affluent than the other. One might include the less affluent individual, if he is an individual who is not worried about personal liability, with the corporation as the general partners of the limited partnership. In this event, if all of the other Internal Revenue requirements were complied with there would be no question but that the partnership would be taxed as a partnership rather than a corporation, no matter how rich or insolvent the individual general partner is, so long as there is an individual in addition to the corporation as one of the general partners.

The Limited Partnership
how and what is limited

What is a theatrical limited partnership agreement? What is a partnership agreement? What is limited about this agreement? The partnership agreement is an agreement between the general partner (the producer) and the limited partners (the investors) which agreement sets forth their duties and obligations with respect to each other concerning the production of the play and their respective rights in the play and the proceeds from the play. The word "limited," as we have previously noted, refers to something that should be limited, namely the investors' liability, and if the agreement is properly drafted and the law is complied with, will, in fact, be limited to the extent of the investment (plus the possible overcall if provided for), and no more. An investor who is a limited partner need not be concerned that he will be personally responsible if the producer goes over budget and spends more money than he has raised.

In a partnership other than a limited partnership, that is in a general partnership, each partner is responsible to the creditors for all of the partnership obligations. This kind of obligation is assumed solely by the general partner in a limited partnership agreement, and this is one of the things that distinguishes the general partner from the limited partners in that the general partner's liability is not limited but is unlimited.

In exchange for the limitation of liability of the investors, you, as the producer, are given the right to be the "chief" and solely in charge of all the decisions of the partnership. The general partner has all of the say-so in all respects, and as the producer, you are in a position to make all of the business and artistic decisions without any interference from the limited partners. As producer, if you want to listen to a limited partner's advice, you may do so or you may ignore such advice and do as you please.

legal publication

In order to insure that the liability of the investors is limited, the law must be strictly complied with. The law of the State of New York provides that a Certificate of Limited Partnership must be filed in the County Clerk's office of the county in which the principal office of the partnership is located, and that a copy of this Certificate or a digest of this Certificate must be published once a week for six consecutive weeks in two newspapers within the county. One of the newspapers designated for publication is the New York Law Journal, and the other one may be any one of many newspapers authorized to publish legal advertisements. A Certificate of Limited Partnership or a digest of the Certificate of Limited Partnership must contain the name, address, and amount of the investment of each limited partner, in addition to the other items in the Certificate. Publishing a large list of investors' names for six weeks in two newspapers can be an expensive outlay for a company operating on the limited budget of an off-Broadway production. If the company has between 50 and 60 investors, the legal advertising bill will range between $650 and $800, more or less depending upon the other terms and provisions of the Certificate.

There are all kinds of people giving all kinds of advice on how to save legal advertising money, and the advice is usually wrong. You may accomplish the result of saving money in some instances, at the same time defeating your very purpose in that you do not give the investors the limited liability to which they are entitled, but rather expose them to the liability of a general partner.

I have in the past had occasion to examine a certain widely used joint venture agreement which purported to protect the investors and which, in fact, did not accomplish this purpose. The investors may never have had to reach into their pocket for additional money because the general partner did not go over budget, or if he did, he personally paid the difference, but there is no good reason why a limited partner should even be exposed to the possibility of being hurt in that fashion. When he parts with his money, if the investor buys nothing else he should at least get a limitation of his liability to the amount of money which he actually invests and no more.

assignments

There is one method which may be used to greatly reduce the cost of legal advertising in some instances. We earlier learned that an option agreement may be assigned, that is, transferred from one party to another. The same is true of a limited partner's share of a limited partnership. Since it is only necessary to publish the names of limited partners, it is possible to provide that most of the investors will be assignees (persons to whom an assignment is made) of a limited partner. An assignee of a limited partner in effect acquires the right to share in the profits the same as if the party were actually a limited partner. The significant difference between an assignee of a limited partner and a limited partner is the fact that an assignee may not demand to see the books and records of the partnership. There are ways of circumventing this limitation. The assignee of a limited partner would of course enjoy the same limited liability that the limited partner enjoys since he acquires his rights from the limited partner. If most of the investors in a show are willing to take an assignment for their investment, and the production has just one or two limited partners who assign their interests to other investors to the extent of their investment, then it is only necessary to publish the names, addresses, amount of investment, and percentage interest of these one or two limited partners. The legal advertising for an off-Broadway production with one or two limited partners would be in the neighborhood of $250. There may be any number of investors who take an assignment for their share, and their names need not be published.

May I strongly and urgently caution you, however, that if your investors become assignees rather than limited partners, it should be done under the guidance of a knowledgeable attorney. There are certain tax ramifications and undesirable consequences which may result if improperly handled. It ought to be done in such a way that your investors end up with everything important that they would otherwise end up with in the same fashion as if they were limited partners. This is possible but only if it's done properly.

Limited Partnership Agreement Form

There is no standard form of theatrical partnership agreement. There is a form commonly used by many attorneys, which form was originally intended for Broadway productions. Even for a Broadway show, this particular form must be adapted by adding particular provisions at the end which are especially applicable to the particular show. For an off-Broadway production, this form is sometimes adapted to the situation, however, it is usually necessary to make so many additions and changes in this form that it is deemed inadvisable to use it under most circumstances. I often use a different form for an off-Broadway production than for a Broadway production; the off-Broadway form being a less complicated version.

profit sharing

Almost all limited partnership agreements used in theatre have some things in common. One common thing is that almost all provide that the investors in the show will receive fifty (50%) percent of the profits of the producing company which includes not only the profits earned at the box-office, but also the profits earned by the company from all sources, including the profits from subsidiaries. They are rare, but there are some producers who will give the limited partners sixty (60%) percent of the profits and retain only forty (40%) percent for themselves. On the other hand, there are producers who under certain circumstances, limit the investors' share of the profits to fifty (50%) percent of the profits from only the gross box-office receipts, and they do not give the investors any share in the subsidiary rights, or give only a limited interest in some of the subsidiary rights. This is a more common practice if the producer is producing a play by a universally well-known author or composer. This may happen when the producer knows he will have to turn away some of the money offered, and that there will be many persons clamoring to invest in the production. The producer may know that there will be no problem selling the investors shares without giving away an interest in the subsidiary rights. This is most assuredly an off-Broadway rarity. It does happen sometimes on Broadway and there have been those rare occasions when it has happened off-Broadway.

budget — capitalization

The agreement will provide that the general partner has acquired the right to produce the show and that he is assigning all of these rights to the partnership which will later be formed. The general partner or the general partner's attorney will receive the money as it is invested by the investors and will hold it in a trust account until enough money is raised, as set forth in the agreement, to produce the show, at which time the partnership will be formed. At this point the money may be released and used by the producer for the production. If the partnership agreement so provides, an investor may give the producer the right to use his money invested before the total budget is raised; however, this is not advisable from the investor's point of view as this could expose him to the liability of a general partner. For this reason, most investors will not grant the right.

The money is held and is not released for production use until enough money is raised to produce the show. "Enough money" to produce the show is a different amount than you ideally would like to have for the production. If you know that you can produce the show with a small reserve on $35,000, but that it would be much preferable to do it with $40,000 and a larger reserve, you will have a budget of $40,000 with a provision in the agreement that you can produce the show if, as and when you've raised $35,000 or an amount between $35,000 and $40,000. You may be faced with the alternative of doing the show with $35,000 or something between $35,000 and $40,000, or not doing the show at all. You may have a commitment either from a theatre, a star, or a director at the time that you have actually raised $35,000. You may be faced with the possibility of finally capitalizing at $35,000 or losing the theatre, star, or director if you wait to raise the additional amount to bring your capitalization up to $40,000. Or you may discover that you can raise $35,000 and not one cent more.

If you do finally capitalize for less than the larger amount that you originally sold the shares for, then instead of returning money to the investors, each limited partner will end up with an additional percentage of the show for his investment. That is, a limited partner would invest $800 for a one percent interest in the profits of a $40,000 show, or would invest $700 for a one percent interest in the profits of a $35,000 show. The producer originally starts selling one percent of the profits for $800. If he later decides to capitalize the show for $35,000, then the $800 investment would purchase 1.14% of the net profits of the production, and the investor would receive this share. An investor is investing a fixed dollar amount. In this case, the investor may get more than one percent for an $800 investment but may not get less than one percent for $800.

The reserve is a necessary part of every budget because it is most rare that a show will do sold-out business immediately after it opens. Even with rave reviews, it sometimes takes three to four weeks or more for the word of mouth to catch on and for the tickets to start disappearing from the racks. However, a producer faced with the possibility of doing the show with a smaller reserve, or not doing the show at all, may wisely choose the former alternative.

abandonment

Of course the limited partnership agreement will provide that the producer may abandon the production at any time. This is a necessary requirement, as it is sometimes essential to abandon the production before opening night. In the event of abandonment, the only obligation to the investors is the return of all monies on hand and an accounting for the other monies spent on the production.

payment of profits

The agreement will provide that the profits will be paid to the investors monthly, after payment of all debts, and after establishment and maintenance of a cash reserve in a given amount. The excess, if any, is then paid to the limited partners until they have recouped their original investment. With an off-Broadway show, the cash reserve can vary between $3,000 and $10,000. The maintenance of a cash reserve is important to get through some of those bad weeks which can sneak in when least expected and also when very much expected. The agreement will also provide that the limited partners may examine the books of account of the partnership, and that the general partner will furnish accounting statements as required by law.

return of profits to company

The agreement will also provide that if moneys have been paid to the limited partners during the run of the show and money is needed, then the general partner may request that the limited partners return first the profits, and then the capital (the original investment) that was returned to them up to the total amount that they had initially invested in the show. One can understand that it is possible for a production to do good business for six or eight months —such good business that some of the money is returned to the investors—and then hit a slow, slack season when the production, having used up the reserve, really needs the money to stay alive which it previously paid out to the partners. Under such circumstances, the money paid to the investors would have to be returned by them if requested by the producer. Of course, it goes without saying that to the extent that the limited partners return any profits paid to them, the general partner must also return a proportionate share of the profits which have been paid to him.

producer's fee and cash office charge

In addition to the share of the profits to which the producer is entitled, the producer will also receive a producer's fee and a "cash office charge." The cash office charge is to reimburse the producer for the expenditures by him in maintaining an office (which includes stationery, rent, secretary, etc.) for the play.

The producer need not have a separate office but may, if he wishes, use his apartment and still collect the cash office charge. It is not uncommon for a producer to install a second telephone line in his apartment and use the apartment as the office of the producing company. The producer also need not use the office exclusively for the production. For that matter, the producer himself need not work solely and exclusively on the production, but may at the same time produce more than one show or may at the same time be engaged in another business.

The producer's fee for an off-Broadway show is usually most nominal. It may be a weekly fee of 1% or 2% of the gross box-office receipts, or it may be a fixed fee usually ranging between $75 and $100 per week. In the event there are two producers, they may share a fee which is as much as $150 a week. The cash office charge is usually an amount of $50 or $75 each week, but may, under certain circumstances, be $100 per week.

The amount of the producer's fee and the amount of the cash office charge are most usually related to the amount of the total budget of the show. A show budgeted at $30,000 would in all probability make a payment to the producer as his fee which is far less than the payment to the producer as his fee for a show budgeted for $60,000. The cash office charge would likewise be a variable depending upon the amount of the total budget.

bonds and bond deals

The limited partnership agreement will probably provide that under certain circumstances the limited partners may, in lieu of investing money, deposit a bond with Actors' Equity Association or other organizations. There may also be a provision for the deposit of a bond by a limited partner or other person under such circumstances that the person who puts up the bond money will get his money back prior to any money being paid to the limited partners. It is usually provided that such an arrangement will not reduce the limited partners' interest in the profits. Thus a person putting up bond money under such circumstances will not receive a share of the limited partners' profits in exchange for the bond, but must be compensated either from the general partner's share of the profits or in some other fashion by the general partner.

Something should be said at this point about bond deals and bond dealers. Very often a limited partnership agreement provides that a person, whether he be a limited partner or not, may deposit the amount of the Equity bond or may make other advance deposits under very special arrangements. In exchange for this advance on the bonds, the agreement may provide that the party is entitled to the show's first receipts, but that no arrangements may be made which would reduce the share of the limited partners. This means that in exchange for the bond investment, you cannot give a share of the limited partners' profits commensurate with the investment. For that matter, you cannot give any share of the limited partners' profits in exchange for such an investment. What will generally happen is that the general partner will agree that the first money received will be used to reimburse the person to the extent of the bond, and that the person putting up the bond will receive a share of the general partner's profits.

Actually most productions are budgeted so that the bond money need not be used, thus if the agreement provides that the bond money is to be returned to the party who furnished it unless he has been reimbursed to that extent by the company, it can readily be seen that the party making such an investment has much less risk than the other limited partners. The entire capitalization may be spent and the bonds may remain intact to be returned in full to the bond dealer. When I say that the partnership agreement usually provides that the investor who puts up bond money may not reduce the share of the limited partners' investment by so doing, I am stating what is the usual case. Of course, the limited partnership agreement may provide otherwise. So long as it's not contrary to public policy and all of the limited partners agree to it, it's possible to provide anything in the agreement. To my way of thinking it would be most unfair to treat one limited partner differently than another limited partner. Thus to arrange that one limited partner would get his money back first, simply because his money was used for the bond, rather than all of the limited partners getting their money returned to them at the same time is unfair.

The provision in the printed form of the limited partnership agreement that is used by many attorneys for a Broadway production provides that the investment in bonds is, in a sense, treated like any other investment, in that in the event that the partnership pays any amounts covered by the bond obligation so that the bond remains intact for the bond owner, the bond owner must pay the same amount of cash to the partnership to reimburse the partnership for picking up this obligation. This kind of an arrangement seems most fair; however, almost all of the agreements have the added provision that any bond deal may be made (fair or not) so long as it does not reduce the share of the limited partners.

What bonds are we talking about, and what amounts of money are involved? The Actors' Equity Association bond is in the amount of two weeks salary for all of the Equity personnel plus a $50 bookkeeping charge. In the event that the bond is not used to pay salaries, then the entire bond including the bookkeeping charge is returned to the producing company.

The Association of Theatrical Press Agents and Managers will likewise expect a bond in the amount of two weeks salary. If you are producing a musical, the American Federation of Musicians, Local 802, will insist upon a bond in the amount of one week's salary for all of the musicians. The theatre's advance deposit is in the nature of a bond; however, it is usually non-returnable in that the amount on deposit is used to pay the rental during the last weeks of the lease. In any event, as was previously noted, the theatre will expect an advance deposit of between three and six weeks of rental, and may expect between $150 and $500 to cover any unpaid bills or damages to the theatre.

Beware of the fact that there are operating in the theatrical area, bond dealers who are waiting around to make the bond investment for almost any show on the most onerous terms. If a production is so nearly capitalized that all that is needed is another $3000 or $4000, and that last $3000 or $4000 is getting difficult to obtain, it seems at first blush like a very prudent thing to have someone come in and furnish the bond money. The problem is that most of these people who are willing to furnish bond money don't want to take the risk that is inherent in theatrical investing; they want an edge, an advantage over everyone else who is making an investment, plus the fact that they expect to get a greater remuneration than the other investors. This happens because the bond wheeler-dealers know how desperate a producer may be to get the last few dollars, the final money to complete the capitalization of the show, and they take advantage of this fact. Be cautious of any bond deal. Know that when you start out to raise your money, you will need enough money to cover the bonds. When someone approaches you to make it easier for you to get your bond money, make certain you don't part with more than you should in exchange for a quick bond dollar.

overcall and loans

The partnership agreement may provide that in addition to the amount that the limited partners are investing, they may be called upon to make an additional investment up to ten (10%) percent, or sometimes up to fifteen (15%) percent or twenty (20%) percent of the amount of their original investment. This is known as an overcall.

In the event that additional money is needed above the total capitalization (and above the overcall if it is provided for in the agreement) the general partner or others may furnish this money and may do so as a loan which may be entitled to be repaid prior to the return of any of the contributions of the limited partners. It is usually provided that the partnership cannot incur any expenses in connection with any such loan, nor can the percentage of the limited partners' profits be affected by such an arrangement. It is for the general partner to reimburse the person for the loan.

option provisions in agreement

It is most usual for a partnership agreement to contain the provisions of the option agreement, particularly the amount that was spent for the option, the terms of the option, and the arrangement with respect to subsidiary rights. Having discussed subsidiary rights in connection with the option agreement, we know that this term as commonly used refers to not only the right to produce the play in other places and in other media, but as well is used to refer to the production's interest in the profits which accrue to the author from his sale or other disposition of the subsidiary rights.

termination of partnership

It is provided in the agreement that the partnership will terminate when all rights in the play have been exhausted, or upon the death, retirement, or insanity of an individual general partner or the dissolution of a corporate general partner. Upon termination of the partnership, the agreement will provide that all of the bills will first be paid, and then a reserve will be established for payment of any bills which later accrue. Thereafter the limited partners will first have the amount of their respective investment returned to them, and if there is any money left over, it will be shared in the same percentage that the general partners and the limited partners share the profits of the company; that is, usually with the limited partners receiving fifty (50%) percent and the general partners receiving the other fifty (50%) percent.

miscellaneous

Of course ther are some other standard provisions which usually appear in partnership agreements. We've already discussed an arbitration clause with respect to an option, and the limited partnership agreement will also contain such a provision. The agreement may be executed in counterparts, all of which taken together shall be deemed one original, and there will be a statement to this effect in the agreement. This means that all of the parties need not sign the same copy of the agreement.

The agreement will also provide that the limited partners grant a general partner a power of attorney to sign the Certificate of Limited Partnership, any amended Certificates, and the Certificate of Dissolution of the Partnership, so that no matter how many limited partners there are, the Certificate of Limited Partnership, which must be filed with the County Clerk, need not personally be signed by each of these limited partners. After all of the money is raised, the Certificate of Limited Partnership is drafted and it would be a totally unnecessary chore to have to have the Certificate signed by each investor.

A limited partnership agreement sometimes provides that in the event the producer wants to produce an additional company of the play, such as a tour or a London production, he may retain the profits from the original company over and above the reserve, until he has accumulated enough money to produce the additional company. If the profits are used for this purpose, it will in effect mean that the investors in the original company will become investors in the additional company with their profits from the original company.

One must bear in mind that the partnership agreement is prepared prior to a producer's raising any money. The partnership, however, is not actually formed until all of the money for the production is raised. The actual formation of the partnership usually takes place at the time that the Certificate of Limited Partnership is filed with the County Clerk. Thus we have been considering a limited partnership agreement to establish a producing company, which agreement will be prepared ahead of time but will only become effective upon completion of the money raising, at the time that the entity actually comes into existence.

4   Raising the Money

The option has been negotiated and prepared—you've signed it, parted with your money, may also have a co-producer, and now own a property. You have six months or a year in which to do all of the things necessary to get the play on stage for your opening night. Your most pressing concern now becomes "money."

If you have an attractive can of beans, there is always a purchaser for it. I do know of instances where very successful shows have had long hard struggles to raise the necessary production money; however, there is always the consolation that the good scripts do eventually get the necessary money and do get produced. Worse than not getting the money is seeing a production that has raised its money badly produced. If a play, a person, a book, or a movie does not live up to its potential, it is heartbreaking.

Budgets

Raising money involves a number of things, and before we can intelligently consider them it is necessary to obtain budgets, so that we know how much has to be raised and how it will be spent. You will need a pre-production budget which will set forth the total amount of money necessary to produce the play including the reserve, and you will need a weekly budget which will set forth the anticipated usual expenses during each week. The weekly budget will make it easy to determine what percentage of the theatre must be sold each week in order for you to break even, and what the potential profit would be if the show does "sold out" business.

The pre-production budget for an off-Broadway show is in all probability going to be between $25,000 and $65,000. If it is substantially less than $25,000, you probably made a mistake in your computations. If it is substantially more than $65,000, you had better worry a second time about whether or not you want to produce the show. There are very few off-Broadway theatres in the City of New York that can bring in enough business that will justify a pre-production budget in excess of $65,000. It just isn't good business.

After preparing the weekly budget, if you see that the production does not break even at about 50% or 60% of capacity, again you'd better either recompute the budget or start looking for a different property. The concept of sold-out business is a nice idea to envision, but it happens so rarely in the business that a producer is wise in assuming that if he's doing 75% or 80% of capacity, he's doing well. Even the smash sold-out shows are rarely sold-out for every performance every night of the week unless it's an extremely small theatre. It's just that there are certain nights during the week such as Tuesday or Wednesday, and rainy or snowy nights, when the demand is less, and then too some of the less desirable seats are sometimes hard to move.

In all probability, the budgets which you have prepared will show that the total amount invested may be recovered if the production does sold out business for between eight and sixteen weeks. If your figures are considerably different than this, once again recompute what you've done until now.

If you have never seen a budget, don't know what a budget looks like, and don't know how to prepare a budget, it is strongly urged that you make contact with a good general manager—there are several in the business—and you will need one eventually anyhow. There is a more detailed discussion in a later chapter of a general manager and his duties. A general manager will be able to prepare the budgets for you that you will need, and you will be able to relax knowing that they are prepared as they should be.

Typical Budgets

So that you have some idea of what a budget looks like, there is set forth here typical budgets for a dramatic off-Broadway play and typical budgets for a musical off-Broadway play. Please again bear in mind that this is not an average budget, since there is no such thing as an average budget. Also bear in mind that many of the items on the budget change weekly or monthly, and those items that don't change weekly or monthly could have changed since these budgets were prepared.

DRAMATIC PLAY

PRODUCTION BUDGET—199 SEAT THEATRE

PHYSICAL PRODUCTION & RENTALS

Costumes	$ 1250.00
Props	350.00
Sets	2500.00
Rehearsal space	500.00
Scenery & lighting	600.00
	$ 5200.00

FEES

Designers	$ 1250.00
Director	1000.00
Author	650.00
Accountant	1000.00
Attorney	2500.00
Manager	750.00
	$ 7150.00

REHEARSAL EXPENSE

Stage Manager (4 x 185)	$ 740.00
Stage Manager's expenses	75.00
Press Agent (2 x 275)	550.00
Actors (4) (4 x 150)	2400.00
Understudies (2) (1 wk)	200.00
Crew	450.00
Scripts	150.00
Producer	400.00
Box Office (1 wk)	150.00
	$ 5115.00

ADVERTISEMENT & PROMOTION

Printing, posters and mailing	$ 450.00
Newspaper advertising	5000.00
Press Agent Expenses	200.00
Photographs and Signs	300.00
	$ 5950.00

BOND AND ADVANCE PAYMENTS

ATPAM Bond	$ 550.00
Theatre Deposit	3000.00
Equity	1990.00
	$ 5540.00

GENERAL & ADMINISTRATION

Telephone	$ 300.00
Insurance	500.00
Hospitalization and Welfare	400.00
Office	250.00
Payroll taxes	800.00
Legal Advertising	750.00
Tickets and Programs	350.00
NYC Rent Tax	40.00
Miscellaneous	500.00
	$ 3890.00
	$32845.00
Contingency	$ 7155.00
Total	$40000.00

DRAMATIC PLAY

WEEKLY OPERATING BUDGET—199 SEAT THEATRE

($11,230.00 Gross)

SALARIES

Stage Manager	$ 185.00
Actors (4) ($165.00)	660.00
Understudies (2) ($100.00)	200.00
General Manager	250.00
Press Agent	275.00
Crew (2)	225.00
	$1795.00

ROYALTIES & FEES

Designer	$ 50.00
Attorney	100.00
Author (5%)	547.00
Director (2%)	218.00
Accountant	110.00
Producer's fee	150.00
Office fee	100.00
	$1275.00

RENT

Theatre — Complete (All personnel)	$1400.00

DEPARTMENTAL COST

Stage Manager expenses	$ 100.00
Wardrobe	50.00
Sets	50.00
	$ 200.00

OTHER

Union Benefits	$ 200.00
Box office expenses	50.00
NYC Rent Tax	37.00
Cast food	30.00
Telephone	75.00
Insurance	50.00
Payroll taxes	300.00
	$ 742.00

PUBLICITY

Printing and photos	$ 50.00
Advertisements	2500.00
Press Agent Expenses	50.00
	$2600.00
Total Weekly Budget	$8012.00

OFF-BROADWAY MUSICAL
PRODUCTION BUDGET—299 SEAT THEATRE

REHEARSAL

Actors (7 x 160 x 4)	$ 4480.00
Stage Manager (1 x 200 x 6)	1200.00
ASM (1 x 20 x 4)	80.00
Musicians (3 x 300 x 2)	1800.00
Pianist (1 x 400 x 5)	2000.00
Press Agent (2 x 400)	800.00
Producer (1 x 200 x 6)	1200.00
Scripts	300.00
Rehearsal Space (3 x 200)	600.00
Production Assistant (1 x 125 x 6)	750.00
General and/or Co. Man. (1 x 300 x 6)	1800.00
Box office (1 week)	300.00
	$ 15310.00

FEES

Author (Basic rights)	500.00
Composer	1500.00
Lyricist	1500.00
Director	2000.00
Choreographer	1000.00
Musical Director	1000.00
Scenic & Lighting Designer	1500.00
Costume Designer	1000.00
Orchestrations	1000.00
Legal	4000.00
Accounting	1000.00
Music Copying	800.00
General Manager	1000.00
	$ 17800.00

PHYSICAL

Lighting	800.00
Costumes	3000.00
Props	600.00
Scenery	5000.00
Take-in and Hanging	750.00
	$ 10150.00

OTHER

Office Expenses	700.00
Payroll Tax	2000.00
Legal Advt. & Disb.	1000.00
Insurance	1000.00
Hospitalization	1000.00
Tickets & Programs	800.00
NYC Rent Tax (5% of Rehearsal rent)	100.00
	$ 6600.00

PROMOTION

Advertising	$ 5000.00
Photos, Signs, Etc.	1000.00
Printing & Mailing	1000.00
Art Work, Layout, logo, etc.	1000.00
Misc.	2000.00
	$ 10000.00

BONDS

Theatre (6 wks at 2000)	12000.00
AEA	2640.00
Showcase actors	1700.00
ATPAM	1500.00
Utility Bond Theatre	1000.00
	$ 18840.00
Pre Contingency Total	$ 78700.00
Contingency	$ 21300.00
Total	$100000.00

OFF-BROADWAY MUSICAL

WEEKLY OPERATING BUDGET—299 SEAT THEATRE

ROYALTIES AND FEES

Authors — 6%	$ 600.00
Scenic and Lighting Designers	100.00
Costume Designer	75.00
Director	200.00
Audit Fee	150.00
Legal Fee	100.00
	$ 1225.00

SALARIES

Cast (7 @ 160)	$ 1120.00
Stage Manager	200.00
ASM	20.00
Understudies (2)	320.00
Musicians (1 @ 400, 3 @ 300)	1300.00
Crew: Electrician	200.00
Props, Stage Crew, Wardrobe	200.00
House Staff: Ushers (2)	75.00
Clerical & House Mgr.	150.00
Box Office Treasurer	300.00
Press Agent	400.00
General & Co. Manager	400.00
	$ 4685.00

PUBLICITY & PROMOTION

Press Expenses	$ 100.00
Newspaper	2000.00
Photos, Signs, Misc.	100.00
	$ 2200.00

THEATRE & MISC.

Cash Office Charge	$ 150.00
Electric (including rentals)	100.00
Set/props	50.00
Office & Box Office	60.00
House Supplies	60.00
Wardrobe — Clean & Repair	200.00
Cast food	50.00
Rent	2000.00
Utilities	150.00
Tickets & Programs	100.00
Insurance	150.00
Payroll taxes	500.00
NYC Rent tax	100.00
Union benefits — pension, Welfare	300.00
Other Misc.	200.00
	$ 4170.00
Total	$12280.00

How to raise the money for the show is an easy question for me to answer. The answer is simply, "I don't know." Some people try auditions; they sometimes work. Some people try friends; they some-

times work. Some people send out copies of the script; that sometimes works. Some people try a combination of these; that sometimes works. What works for you, you will have to discover after
you attempt to raise the money and examine the results.

Backers' Auditions

Backers' auditions are sometimes held, where potential investors
are invited to a sampling of the play. The audition may take place
in someone's home, in a hotel room rented for that purpose, or in
some other public place such as a restaurant. The Belasco Room at
Sardi's has become a favorite auditioning place; however, some off-
Broadway producers do not have the front money to spend on so
elaborate an audition.

You may plan on serving alcoholic beverages or coffee and cake.
Nice surroundings may be helpful in getting people to part with their
money and perhaps the drinks may also help; however, nothing is
quite as important as what happens on stage.

The backers' audition may consist of actors performing the parts,
or as is often done with musicals, the author may give the story line,
and the composer and author sing the musical numbers.

While I'm not sure whether serving alcoholic beverages is more
important than serving coffee, I am nevertheless quite sure of two
things. Firstly, you should start on time. It's unfair to the people
who arrive on time to keep them waiting. When you want people
to invest in a show, it's advisable not to get them angry with a wait.
If you are serving drinks, of course it's all right to have a half hour
for the drinks before the presentation. A half hour doesn't mean 45
minutes or an hour.

Secondly, the presentation should not be more than an hour or an
hour and 15 minutes. Some producers find it hard to cut a play as they
are so certain that every line is important. This is especially true if the
author is the producer. Backers who come to backers' auditions, for
the most part, do not want to sit through the entire play but will
settle for a condensed version.

Before or after the presentation, the producer usually makes a short speech in which he tells a little bit about himself, about the budget, and answers any questions that might come up. This presentation by the producer also must be short. Short means no more than five or six minutes.

Don't count on very many people at the conclusion of the audition pulling out their checkbooks and writing you a check. It doesn't happen very often that they do. What should happen is that sometime within two or three days after the audition, you will follow up each one of the people who attended by telephoning them to see if they are interested in investing in the play. This means, of course, that you must have taken the names, addresses, and telephone numbers of all of the people who attended the audition. If you have interested people who want to invest, of course you must question them about any friends they might have who might be interested and whom you could invite to the next audition.

There are occasions when producers will send out large mailings from mailing lists which they have assembled or which they have purchased. The mailing lists usually consist of people who have previously invested in shows. For the most part, this method of raising money is not to be recommended. You will find that you may get people to a backers' audition because they are curious, are seeking entertainment, and have nothing to do that evening. Let's face the fact that most people, not all mind you, but most people invest in shows because of some personal connection with it in some way. They either know the producer, the author, the star, or a friend of theirs knows someone who is part of the show. There is usually some kind of a personal involvement on the part of most off-Broadway investors rather than the investment coming as a business venture.

You will have to decide how small an investment you will be willing to accept. If one percent of the show sells for $600, that is if you have a $30,000 budget, you will probably be willing to accept an investment for one-half percent at $300, but may not wish to bother with an investment of $150. Many producers will bother with investments in any reasonable amount and would certainly consider $150 to be a reasonable amount.

It must appear evident that I don't know exactly how you raise the money. I do, however, know for certain what you must do before you can raise the money. This, of course, brings us to a discussion of the Securities and Exchange Commission and the Attorney General of the State of New York.

The Securities and Exchange Commission

I really think I spoke too soon when I previously commented that no subject is surrounded with so much confusion as subsidiaries. I do believe, upon reflection, that the requirements of the Securities and Exchange Commission, which is usually referred to as the "SEC," elicits even more confusion. This should not be so because the SEC regulations and SEC requirements setting forth whether or not SEC filing is necessary are not really that complicated. It's just that people believe what they want to believe. The SEC regulates the issuance or sale of securities. Although a security is commonly thought of as a stock or a bond, they have interpreted the sale of a limited partnership interest in a producing company organized to produce a play, to be a sale of a "security." Although the requirements as to the necessity for a filing are not that complicated, an SEC filing itself is somewhat complicated. Since producers want to avoid the trouble, time and expense of a filing if they can, they are too often ready to believe anything that they might hear which would serve as an excuse for them to not file with the SEC.

If you intend to raise money outside the State of New York, that is, if you intend to go to, send mail to, telephone, or in any other way approach someone in a state other than the State of New York to raise money, and if this consists of a public offering, then you must file with the SEC. A public offering means exactly what it sounds like it means. It means that you are offering to sell an interest in the limited partnership (or other entity) which will be producing the play, to people that you don't know or people that you haven't known. It means someone other than sophisticated investors who may be your intimate friends, or your business associates. And further-more, if there is any question as to whether or not your offering constitutes a public offering, the presumptions which the SEC makes all support the conclusion that it is a public offering.

When the chap across the hall tells you that you need not file with the SEC if you have less than nine investors, don't believe him. When your wife's cousin tells you that you needn't file with the SEC if your production budget is less than $25,000, don't believe him. When your actor friend, who just produced a show down in the Village tells you that there is a way to avoid filing with the SEC if you give the New Jersey resident who's going to invest the money a New York residence for the purpose of the agreement, don't believe him. It's hardly worth the risk in view of the fact that amongst other possible penalties, if you raise money in interstate commerce by a public offering, and you do not file with the SEC, you, as the producer, are personally liable for the money you have raised. Understand that means that you may raise the full $30,000, open your show, get bombed by the reviews, close the show, and then have to reach into your pocket and come up with $30,000 to return to the investors. Is this really worth the risk of not filing with the SEC when you should have done so?

Since the budget for an off-Broadway production would be less than $300,000, our discussion will be concerned with an "Exemption from Registration under Regulation A" rather than what is known as a full registration. Don't be misled by the term, "Exemption from Registration." The term is somewhat misleading because one might assume that if you are "exempt" there is nothing you need do. This, of course, is not the case. Under the circumstances you will be exempt from registration under the Securities Act. Registration is a complicated procedure, so the exemption is some concession. You must, however, file certain documents with the SEC which they must accept for filing for you to obtain your exemption from registration.

What must one file with the SEC? One must file four copies of a Notification under Regulation A, which is a document which gives certain information about you as the issuer. The Notification will state where you will be conducting business; information on persons with whom you are affiliated; the name of your counsel; whether or not you have ever been convicted of a crime or guilty of a post-office fraud; whether you have been declared a bankrupt; any connection you may have with underwriters; the states in which you intend to raise money;

information on any other offerings by you during the last year; and any other offerings contemplated by you. This document will be prepared by your attorney and will be signed by you, and four copies will be submitted to the SEC together with four copies of your proposed offering circular, four copies of your proposed limited partnership agreement, four copies of all sales material you intend to use; and four copies of other pertinent documents. Depending upon how busy the SEC is, within three to four weeks after the submission of this material to them, a letter will be forwarded to your attorney informing him of either the acceptance as filed, or the changes requested by them before they will accept the submission for filing.

You will notice that I referred to an "acceptance" for filing rather than an "approval" of filing. The Securities and Exchange Commission is careful to make this important distinction in that they do not approve or disapprove of the filing. They accept what is submitted for filing or they may reject it. In effect, if it does not meet with their approval they will not accept it for filing, although they are careful to point out that they do not ever officially approve of what is filed.

You may not use any written material in connection with the offering that has not been filed with the SEC. You must give an offering circular to each prospective investor. Sometimes a producer tries to be cute and surreptitiously prepares an attractive brochure which has not been filed with the SEC which he mails or distributes together with the offering circular. Every client of mine knows that he must not do this, and on the one occasion when a client without my knowledge sneaked something in to a large mailing and it was discovered, the consequences were not pleasant. Again, it's easier to properly file with the SEC than to run the risk of not filing if it is required, or to avoid the SEC requirements.

The offering circular which must be filed with the SEC for an exemption from registration is patterned after a form which was arrived at as a result of discussions between the SEC and the League of New York Theatres. The offering circular presently used leaves much to be desired from a theatrical point of view, but is a great improvement over the offering circular previously used. The formerly used offering circular had no relationship to theatre but was originally intended for use by almost every other type of business, such as oil companies, steel companies and the like.

The SEC takes the position that they merely want a full disclosure of all pertinent information and that nothing must be misleading. The offering circular now in use certainly could not be considered a document which would encourage investment in a theatrical production. Be that as it may, the offering circular explains some of the terms of the limited partnership agreement such as the division of profits and the fact that the producers will receive a percentage of the net profits without making a financial contribution. It sets forth the risk to the investors including statistics on the percentage of plays during the previous season which resulted in losses to investors; the experience of the producers; the minimum number of performances that the play will have to run in order to recover the initial investment; and what percentage of plays actually ran this long during the previous season. There is information on the play, the author, the director, the cast, the theatre, the scenic designer. There is additional information on the compensation of the general partners, as well as a pre-production budget setting forth how the proceeds of the offering will be used. There is a provision setting forth the estimated weekly budget and what percentage of the gross weekly box-office receipts and of the net receipts will first be paid as expenses off the top to stars, the director, etc. before there are net profits. The offering circular also contains a short discussion of the subsidiary rights and the fact that the investors will receive financial statements.

Following is an example of a typical Offering Circular:

$55,000.00 in Limited Partnership Interests

in

T H E   F I C T I O N A L   C O M P A N Y

A Limited Partnership to be formed to Finance the Play

"MUSICAL FICTION"

(tentative title)

THESE SECURITIES ARE OFFERED PURSUANT TO AN EXEMPTION FROM REGISTRATION WITH THE UNITED STATES SECURITIES AND EXCHANGE COMMISSION. THE COMMISSION DOES NOT PASS UPON THE MERITS OF ANY SECURITIES NOR DOES IT PASS UPON THE ACCURACY OR COMPLETENESS OF ANY OFFERING CIRCULAR OR OTHER SELLING LITERATURE.

THE OFFERING

Daniel Doe and Richard Roe intend to produce the Play, "Fiction." They offer Limited Partnership interests in a Partnership to be formed for that purpose, and they will be the General Partners. They will make no financial contribution but will receive fifty (50%) percent of any net profits. Limited Partners will make the entire financial contribution for which they will receive fifty (50%) percent of any net profits. If there are no net profits, Limited Partners will bear the entire risk of loss to the extent of their respective contributions. Any losses in excess of that amount will be borne by the General Parners. Partners' share in net profits, if any, will be computed only after payment to others of as much as an estimated eight (8%) percent of the gross box-office receipts and deduction of all other expenses from the balance of the gross receipts.

There is no minimum fixed amount that each individual Limited Partner must contribute. An initial contribution of $1,100 entitles a Limited Partner to a one (1%) percent share of any net profits. A maximum of $55,000 will be raised. The Partnership will be formed when $55,000 has been raised, or any amount between $50,000 and $55,000 with which the Producers believe they can present the Play.

The rights and obligations of the General and Limited Partners are set forth in the Limited Partnership Agreement. This must be signed by all subscribers to Limited Partnership interests and may be obtained from Daniel Doe and Richard Roe at 886—33rd Avenue, New York, N.Y., or from John A. Counselor, 46th Street and Park Avenue, New York, N.Y.

TABLE OF CONTENTS

(A Table of Contents will be set forth here)

The date of this Offering Circular is May 1, 1970.

THE RISK TO INVESTORS

(1) The sole business of the Partnership will be the production of the Play. In such a venture the risk of a loss is especially high in contrast with the prospects for any profits. These securities should not be purchased unless the investor is prepared for the possibility of total loss.

(2) Of the plays produced for the New York stage in the 1969-1970 season, 80% resulted in loss to investors.

(3) On the basis of estimated expenses, the Play would have to run for a minimum of 7 weeks (56 performances) off-Broadway to a full capacity house, even to return to Limited Partners their initial contributions. More than 80% of the plays produced for the New York stage in the 1969-1970 season failed to run this long. Of these that did, a mere handful played to capacity audiences.

SUBSCRIPTIONS

Offers to subscribe to Limited Partnership interests are subject to acceptance by the Producers. Contributions must be paid in cash at the time of signing the Limited Partnership Agreement, and will be held in trust by John A. Counselor, Attorney for the Production in a special account with the Wealthy Bank and may not be used until $55,000 has been raised (or such lesser sum in no event below $50,000 which the General Partners regard as sufficient to present the Play) and then only for Partnership purposes. After the Partnership is formed, the funds will thereafter be held by the Producers in a special bank account in trust until such funds are actually employed for pre-production, production, or running expenses of the Production or returned to the investors. The Partnership will not be formed and all contributions will be returned in full if $55,000 has not been received (or such lesser sum in no event below $50,000 which the General Partners regard as sufficient to present the Play) by February 28, 1971, on which date production rights expire, unless the Author wishes to extend them, except to the extent contributions have been expended by consent of individual subscribers who have also waived their right of refund.

An individual subscriber may agree in writing to the use of his contribution prior to formation of the Partnership, or waive his absolute right of full refund in event of an insufficiency of funds on abandonment prior to formation of the Partnership. The Producers will be personally liable to subscribers who agree to immediate use but do not waive full refunds of their contribution.

Investors should note that there is no advantage to entering into these agreements. In fact there is a distinct disadvantage since persons who do so risk loss of their entire investment even if the Partnerhip is never formed.

A subscriber who agrees to earlier use may, under certain circumstances, be personally liable as a General Partner for production debts incurred prior to the date of the formation of the Partnership.

The Producers reserve the right to pay to any individual investor an additional participation in net profits for any reason whatsoever provided such participation is payable solely from the Producers' share and does not affect the percentage of net profits payable to the subscribers.

OVERCALL

There will be no overcall. If additional funds are needed, the General Partners may advance their own funds or obtain necessary funds in a manner that will not reduce the percentage interest of the original Limited Partners in the net profits of the Partnership. Such advances, if made, would be repaid prior to the original Limited contributions.

THE PRODUCERS

The Play will be produced by Daniel Doe and Richard Roe of 886—33rd Avenue, New York, N.Y., who are also promoters and will be the General Partners of the Partnership, with exclusive control of the Production of the Play.

(A brief bio of each of the Producers is herein set forth)

To the extent the Producers advance funds for pre-production ex-expenses, they will be reimbursed upon formation of the Partnership. They have advanced $1500 to date. The Producers may abandon the Production at any time prior to the New York opening for any reason whatsoever.

THE PLAY

(A brief synopsis of the Play is herein set forth)

The show will have a cast of eleven with one set.

The Producers and Authors may make such changes in the Play as they determine.

THE AUTHOR

(A brief bio of the Author is herein set forth)

COMPOSER-LYRICIST

(A brief bio of the Composer-Lyricist is herein set forth)

The Author and Composer in the aggregate will receive six (6%) percent of gross weekly box-office receipts.

THE DIRECTOR

To date no Director has been engaged. Negotiations are presently being carried on with several directors who have expressed interest in the Play, and it is contemplated that the Director who will be selected will be paid a fee of approximately One Thousand ($1,000) Dollars and will receive two (2%) percent of the gross weekly box-office receipts.

THE CAST

To date none of the cast has been selected. It is not contemplated that the compensation of any member of the cast will include a percentage of the gross receipts or net profits.

THE THEATRE

No contract has yet been entered into for a theatre. However, it is estimated that the New York theatre into which the Play will be booked will be a 299 seat house and will have a box-office capacity of $16,750 per week.

SCENIC DESIGNER

To date no scenic designer has been engaged. It is not anticipated that a percentage of the gross weekly box-office receipts or net profits will be paid to the scenic designer.

COMPENSATION OF GENERAL PARTNERS

In addition to their 50% share of any net profits, Daniel Doe and Richard Roe will receive the following compensation and advantages whether or not the Partnership returns a net profit:

As a Producer's management fee $150 in the aggregate, per week commencing two weeks prior to rehearsals until one week after closing.

For furnishing the office space and secretarial services, the General Partners will receive $100 per week for each company presenting the Play. The

office charge shall commence two weeks before the commencement of rehear-
sals and end one week after the close of each company presenting the Play.
The office will be located c/o Daniel Doe and Richard Roe at 886—33rd
Avenue, New York, N.Y., and will not be used exclusively for the Partnership.

To the extent that charges received from the Partnership by the
General Partners for office space or other items furnished by them exceed
their own cost, they will receive additional compensation.

They will receive no compensation, other than stated above, for any
services, equipment or facilities customarily rendered or furnished by a
General Partner, Producer or Author of a theatrical venture; nor will they
receive concessions of cash, property or anything of value from persons ren-
dering services or supplying goods to the Production.

In the event that a Producer finds it necessary to perform any services
of a third person, the Producer may, if he so desires, receive reasonable compensation in the amount that the third person would have received for said
services, for example, in the event that a Producer should act as the Stage
Manager.

The Producers or a company controlled by them may purchase
British Production and subsidiary rights for their own behalf. If this right is
exercised, the Partnership would still receive the percentage due it. The Producers have undertaken that such a sale will only be on fair and reasonable
terms.

USE OF PROCEEDS

The present estimated allocation of proceeds is as follows:

(A pre-production budget is herein set forth)

ESTIMATED WEEKLY BUDGET

The weekly budget for the Play, once it opens in New York, is
estimated at $8,000. Based on a theatre capacity of $16,750 taking into consideration payments to the Authors out of gross receipts, the Play would have
to run a minimum of 7 weeks (56 performances) at full capacity merely to
return to Limited Partners their original investment. Of course there can be
no prediction that the Play will run for that length of time or that it will have
audiences of any specified size for any length of time. Furthermore, additional
production, running or other expenses may be incurred which would increase
the budget and consequently the period of time required to recover invested
capital.

NET PROFITS

"Net Profits" consist of the excess of gross receipts over all "Production", "Running" and "Other" expenses, as those terms are defined in the Limited Partnership Agreement.

As of the date of this Offering Circular, running expenses may be expected to include payments to the Authors and Director amounting to eight (8%) percent of gross weekly box-office receipts. The effect of this is to reduce the Limited Partners' share to 50% of the net profits attributable to roughly 92% of gross box-office receipts. It is not anticipated that anyone else will be engaged at a percentage of gross receipts or net profits.

RETURN OF CONTRIBUTIONS—SHARE OF PROFITS

The Limited Partners as a group will receive 50% of any net profits, each in the proportion his contribution bears to the total Limited Contributions. Any net profits will be distributed only after the off-Broadway opening after all contributions have been repaid and when such distributions will still leave the Partnership with a $10,000 reserve (plus any amounts which the Producers wish to accumulate for the formulation of additional companies to present the Play).

Before net profits are earned, all losses will be borne by the Limited Partners to the extent of their respective contributions. After net profits are earned, the General and Limited Partners will bear losses to the extent of the net profits in proportion to their respective interests. If the partnership liabilities exceed its assets, all partners will be required to return pro rata any net profits distributed to them and if a shortage remains, any repaid contributions as well.

PRODUCTION AND SUBSIDIARY RIGHTS

Under the production contract with the Authors, the Producers have the right to produce and present the Play off-Broadway in New York City. The contract provides that the Authors shall be paid royalties of 6% of the gross box-office receipts less theatre party commissions, discount or cut-rate sales, all admission taxes, any pension and welfare deductions, any subscription fees and actors' fund benefits.

Upon a run of at least 21 off-Broadway performances commencing with the first paid preview performance, the Producers acquire the right to participate in subsidiary rights including motion picture and television.

When the Partnership is formed, the Producers will transfer their interest in the production and the subsidiary rights to the Partnership. The Author has retained the right to dispose of subsidiary rights as he chooses. The Partnership interest in any sale of the rights increases from 10% if the Play runs for 21 off-Broadway performances commencing with the first paid preview performance to 40% if the Play runs for 65 off-Broadway performances commencing with the first paid preview performance, and the interest continues for any disposition made of the rights during the expiration of 15 years after the date of the last public performance off-Broadway.

In the event that the Play opens off-Broadway, the Producers are granted an option to produce a tour of the Play in the United States and Canada and an option to do a production of the Play in the British Isles, all as more fully set forth in the contract, a copy of which is on file at the offices of John A. Counselor, Attorney for the Partnership and is available for inspection by the Limited Partners.

OTHER FINANCING

Except as described above, no person has advanced anything of value toward the production of the Play.

FINANCIAL STATEMENTS

The ultimate issuer of these securities will be the Partnership to be formed. Accordingly, no financial statements are available. The Limited Partners will be furnished with all financial statements required by New York law, which will include, after formation of the partnership, monthly unaudited statements of operations, annual statements which may or may not be audited and also six-month statements personally verified by the Producers. In cases where a long enough period elapses after the initial expenditure of investors' funds, financial statements may have to be furnished even before formation of the Partnership. If the Producers furnish an unaudited annual statement, Limited Partners will not have the benefit of an audit of the Producers' accounts by an independent certified public accountant and will rely wholly upon the Producers' figures for the determination of their share in any net profits.

We have already discussed the Limited Partnership agreement which must be filed with the Offering Circular and the Notification under Regulation A, but it should be noted that four copies of it must be filed with the other documents.

Although the SEC does not pass upon the merits of any security, nor the accuracy or the completeness of an offering circular, or any other selling literature (and you will note that this is stated in bold type on the first page of the offering circular), may I nevertheless strongly urge that you as producer make certain of the accuracy and completeness of any offering circular or selling literature which you use. It's just as easy, in fact easier, to be honest. Dishonesty is not only bad theatre, it's also bad business.

The Attorney General

You must file with the Attorney General of the State of New York before you begin raising money in New York for your show. If it is decided that you are going to raise money only in the State of New York, then you can avoid the SEC filing, but it is still essential that you file with the office of the Attorney General. If you have already filed with the SEC, your filing with the Attorney General is simplified; you just furnish the Attorney General with copies of the documents which you have already filed with the SEC.

It should be noted that most, if not all of the states in the Union, have requirements similar to our New York State Theatre Financing Regulations governing a filing with a State Office before one may offer a security interest for sale. The state laws governing security issues are known as "Blue Sky" laws. You may remember that one of the items of information contained in the Notification under Regulation A which is furnished to the SEC, is a statement setting forth in which states you intend to raise money. It may be necessary to file in each of these states. Consult your attorney, who will advise you as to what filings are necessary and where you must file.

In the case of a filing solely with the Attorney General, if the offering is less than $100,000 (which would be the case of an off-Broadway production), you have your choice of filing a prospectus (an offering circular) and a limited partnership agreement, or you may simply file the limited partnership agreement if it sets forth all of the terms of the agreement you have with the limited partners. Since it should set forth all of such terms, I almost always advise my clients to forego the offering circular and to confine the filing to the limited partnership agreement. The offering circular required by the Attorney General is an added expense and like the SEC offering circular requires the kind of language that is not that helpful in raising money. With the SEC you have no choice but to use an offering circular; however, since there is a choice if it is a filing solely with the Attorney General, I recommend against the use of the offering circular.

If the offering is made to fewer than 26 persons, you may avoid any filing with the Attorney General. To accomplish this, however, each of the investors must expressly waive in writing the right to have offering literature filed with the Attorney General and the right to receive information that would be contained in such an offering circular.

One should also bear in mind that it is not necessary to file with the Attorney General if the offer is made to less than five persons with the sole purpose of obtaining front money to purchase the option or for bond deposits.

Investment Procedure

The producer generally passes out copies of the limited partnership agreement with the offering circular if an offering circular is used. If someone wants to invest in a show, the procedure is simple. The party signs the agreement at the end in one of the two or three places provided for and delivers the partnership agreement together with the check to the producer. The end of the limited partnership agreement usually provides that a person may sign as a limited partner or he may, if he wishes, sign at a different spot and thus give the producer permission to use the money prior to the total budget being raised. In some agreements there is also a provision to the effect that the investor who signs may be making an investment other than in cash.

Actually, the money that the investor is investing is almost always turned over to the producer at the time the limited partnership agreement is signed; however, the agreement may be signed by the investor and the money later delivered to the producer when the producer demands it.

Starting the Company

The producer continues to collect partnership agreements and money until he has enough to produce the show, that is, either the amount of the total production budget or the lesser amount stated in the limited partnership agreement with which the producer may proceed. After all the money has been raised, the partnership is formed by the filing of a Certificate of Limited Partnership. The attorney for the production will prepare a conformed copy of the partnership agreement. A conformed copy is an exact copy in which all of the names of the general partners and the limited partners are listed at the end, in the same fashion that they have signed the agreement. One of these is then sent to each investor.

The Certificate of Limited Partnership mentioned previously is a document which sets forth some of the terms of the partnership, that is the terms with respect to the business of the partnership and the respective interests of the general partners and the limited partners. It must also contain the names, addresses, and amount of the investment of each partner. We have previously discussed this document as the document (or a digest of it) which must be published once a week in two publications for six consecutive weeks. The producing company is in business as a limited partnership when the Certificate is filed, and everything you were doing for the play as an individual or as a joint venture now becomes the business of the partnership. You will assign all of the agreements to the company. The limited partnership assumes all of the obligations of all of the contracts, and takes all of the benefits of the same contracts.

At this time you will reimburse yourself for all expenses made by you for the producing company. The money spent by you to option the property, for legal expenses, and for other items that you give to the company which it can use are reimbursable to you. You may not reimburse yourself for money spent to raise money. Backers' auditions and everything connected with them are the expense of the producer and not the producing company.

You should bear in mind that front money that is furnished by you or someone else may be considered an investment in the producing company to the extent that the money is used for the company and is not returned to the person who furnishes the front money. But to the extent that front money is used for backers' auditions or other money raising, it cannot be considered an investment in the producing company.

5 Obtaining a Theatre

When it looks fairly certain that the money is going to be raised, you spend some of your time shopping for a theatre, although you can't really start shopping for a theatre in earnest until you know exactly when the money will be raised, as the theatre situation changes daily. At the time you prepared the budget, you should have given consideration to the size of the theatre you want and can afford. Naturally the smaller houses cost less, and furthermore the theatres of 199 seats or less have different union requirements than theatres with less than 299 seats but more than 199 seats.

You next speak with the theatre owners or the managers of the theatres in which you are interested to find out what theatres are available and which will fit into your budget requirements. After you settle on the theatre when you have enough money raised that the partnership can be organized and the money used, you start negotiations with the theatre upon the terms that are to be included in the lease. If you don't have enough money raised, and you're certain that the money will be raised, there is nothing to prevent you from either using your own money or using the front money which may have been furnished to you for the purpose of leasing the theatre. Understand, however, that most off-Broadway theatres require between three weeks and six weeks advance deposit or security. This can be as much as $9,000.

Advance Deposit

Sometimes there are all kinds of deals that can be made with respect to the theatre advance, and when I say all kinds of deals I mean exactly that. It is possible to negotiate a lease which provides that after the production has been in the theatre for a certain number of weeks you may reduce the amount that is held on deposit by playing a week or two or three without paying rental. For an example, the lease may provide that after two months you may use up three weeks of the six weeks deposit which the theatre is holding, so that the theatre then will be holding a deposit of only three weeks rental. The deposit is money that is to be used for the last three, four, five or six weeks of the occupancy of the theatre depending upon the size of the deposit.

Four Wall Contract

The first thing you must find out in your negotiations is whether or not you are obtaining a four wall contract, that is, if you are leasing just the theatre or the theatre and added personnel. Some theatres require that you not only lease the theatre, but that you pay them sufficient money to cover the box-office help and the ushers as well as the theatre manager and other personnel which the theatre then furnishes to you. The New York City Department of Licenses takes the position that the box-office personnel must be under the control of the theatre owner, and this kind of an arrangement has some problems in that if the box-office personnel, who are directly responsible for the money, are hired by the theatre, then they are responsible to the theatre. But they are handling your money and are dealing with your money so they should in fact be beholden to you.

Lease or License

Some theatre leases are not a lease at all, but rather a license to use the theatre for certain specific hours during certain specific days. The distinction between a lease and a license is beyond the scope of this book, but for your purpose at this time the differences are not material. The agreement will most likely provide that the theatre is free to license the use of the premises at other hours to other productions; however, they cannot interfere with the production or stage sets and props of the primary occupant at that time. The performance schedule should be the right of the major tenant. As the major tenant, you should not have to work your schedule around any other secondary tenant. The most common use of the theatre at other hours is for children's theatre. It is not unusual for a children's theatre group to use an occupied theatre on Saturday morning or Sunday morning to present a show, without interfering with the sets and props that are in place.

Run of the Show — Moving

The theatre lease or license usually is for the run of the show, which means that the theatre owner cannot put you out of the theatre so long as the play is running, you pay your rent, and comply with the other lease or license terms. By the same token, you must stay in this theatre and cannot move your play to another off-Broadway theatre unless the theatre for some reason loses its license or for some other reason cannot be occupied. Moving can be a very costly expense, so in most instances one should not anticipate a move. I have had producers come to me with the thought in mind that they would open a show in a particular theatre just because it is available, even though they consider the theatre all wrong for this particular play. The plan proposed is to get those great reviews that they know they will get and immediately move the show to a better house. Don't count on doing this! It really doesn't make sense from a business point of view and is near impossible to accomplish. One should also bear in mind that the move from an off-Broadway house to a Broadway house is very expensive and with but one exception, the move has never proven successful.

Of course the theatre owner will make a different deal depending upon how anxious the theatre is to have a particular show in that theatre. In fact, under some circumstances, theatre owners will make an investment in the production to the extent of the advance deposit. There have been instances where theatre owners have even been known to invest beyond this, to the extent that they have actually put money into a show that comes into their theatre.

Stop Clause

Broadway theatre leases have a provision that if the box-office receipts fall below a certain amount of money during any two consecutive weeks, they may ask the production to leave the theatre in order to put another show in. The reason for this is that a Broadway show pays the theatre a percentage of its gross box-office receipts as rental. This is not the case with most off-Broadway theatres, as they are paid a flat fee. When the landlord or the landlord's representative tries to push you into a position which would permit him to put you out of the theatre if your weekly gross box-office receipts fall below a certain amount, resist. He shouldn't complain no matter how much money you lose at the box-office, so long as you pay your rent.

Payment of Rent

The most important part of your deal is that you pay the rent. Almost every lease and license agreement is prepared for the benefit of the landlord. At the beginning it states how much the tenant must pay, and at the end it says that if the tenant complies with the terms of the lease, pays his rent, and abides by the rules of the landlord that he may enjoy peaceful possession of the premises. Everything written in between is for the landlord's benefit. In spite of all the onerous provisions of a lease, and some of them are most onerous, as long as you pay your rent you're not really in too much trouble. The landlord wants to make certain that you do no physical damage to the theatre and that you maintain the premises in reasonably the same condition that they were in at the time that you took possession. He wants to make certain that the rent is paid. These are not unreasonable demands.

Theatre License and Rehearsals

From the point of view of the producer, you should make certain that your lease, license agreement, or whatever, provides that the landlord has a theatre license issued by the Department of Licenses, and that he will maintain the theatre license. This is terribly important to you as it is illegal to perform in front of an audience without a license and the theatre would be worthless to you. You may be able to negotiate with the landlord to permit you to use the premises for rehearsals at a very reduced rate. It is not unusual to pay $100 a week for rehearsals in a theatre where the rental might be $800 a week during performances. It may also be possible for you to negotiate a reduced rate for the theatre during previews. The amount of money that you pay during previews can vary between an amount that is approximately one-half of the usual rental for the theatre and the same amount that is paid during any other paid performances. This is an item for negotiation.

Equity Requirements

You should make certain that the theatre meets all of the requirements of Actors' Equity Association. There must be separate dressing rooms for men and women; there must be toilet facilities available to the members of the cast separate from the audience; there must be wash basins with hot and cold water; there must be a cool drinking water; and thirty inches of dressing room space for each actor. All new theatres hereafter built must be fully air conditioned, that is the playing area and the dressing room area, and they must have separate sanitary facilities backstage for men and women. Not only should the theatre be equipped with everything that is required by Actors' Equity, but the agreement should provide that the theatre must continue to maintain all of these requirements.

The lease or license will sometimes make provision for a deposit of between $150 and $500 to be held by the landlord to insure against breakage, damage to the theatre, and telephone or other charges for which the theatre might be held responsible.

Maintenance and Concessions

In renting a theatre, the producer must always make certain that he examines the light board. It may be necessary in some houses to rent additional lights, and the producer should at least be aware of this before renting the theatre. Rental of lights is the kind of item that may be overlooked when preparing the budget. Who is responsible for maintainence of the air conditioning should always be clearly set forth in the lease.

The producer should try, if possible, to acquire the right to run a concession for the sale of sheet music and records if the play is a musical. Most theatre owners insist on having the right to run all of the concessions and rarely will they part with this right, for it means that the theatre will make extra money from the sale of drinks, checking coats, and the sale of other items.

Advertising

The landlord may, under certain circumstances, try to obtain some control over the advertising, with particular reference to the way that the theatre is mentioned in the ads, and the directions set forth for getting to the theatre. Be careful that you do not let the theatre owner control your ads, as I do not believe that this is a proper function of a theatre owner.

Removal at End and House Seats

Make certain that you have ample time at the conclusion of the lease to remove all of your property. Some leases and some license agreements provide that the theatre owner may have a certain number of house seats for each performance of the show. Almost all lease or license agreements contain a provision stating that the tenant cannot make any arrangements with any unions contrary to the terms which have already been settled upon between that particular theatre and the different unions.

Insurance

The lease will certainly provide that you must maintain liability insurance and fire insurance which must also protect the landlord. As a matter of fact you should bear in mind that the following insurance policies are desirable and some are required. You should consider the following:

Box-office hold-up and safe burglary
    insurance
Box-office Fidelity Bond
New York State Group Disability Benefits
Payroll Hold-up Broad Form Policy
    (This is desirable if you pay the
    cast and crew by cash)
Workmen's Compensation
Theatrical floater for physical props,
    that is, scenery, costumes, rented
    lighting equipment, sound equipment,
    and wardrobe
Extraordinary Risk (This is an Equity
    requirement to cover the salary loss
    of Equity personnel due to injuries
    from acrobatic feats, use of weapons,
    leaps, falls, pyrotechnics, etc.)

Your general manager will assist you in obtaining the insurance necessary and desirable.

Assignability

There is one other provision that should appear in the lease as well as in any other agreement you enter into, if the lease or other agreement are entered into before the producing company is organized. There must be a provision that you can assign the lease or other agreement to the limited partnership or other entity which will later be organized to produce the play. You will remember that we previously discussed an assignment of the option agreement and that it is not unusual to have a provision limiting the assignment to a partnership or corporation in which you are one of the principals. Nor is it unusual to have a provision that you will continue to be responsible for the lease, that is, that you as well as the producing company agree to live up to your end of the bargain.

Location

Serious consideration must be given to location of the theatre. I used to be of the opinion that if you have a good show, that is, if you have something worth seeing, that people will come anywhere in the city to see it. In recent years I've had reason to question this theory. I do know of several theatres that have on more than one occasion had good shows with artistic merit and received good reviews, and in spite of this, the shows were not financially successful.

The Greenwich Village area is probably the most likely area for walk-in trade, that is, people who walk in off the streets to buy tickets. The success of a theatre, of course, is judged by the number of hits and commercially successful shows that have appeared in that theatre. From an artistic point of view, a director may have a different standard for judging a theatre. As the producer of a show, it is important to you that people buy tickets, and the old truism is equally applicable to an off-Broadway production, namely, that it is not good theatre unless there are people watching it.

Bargaining

Bear in mind that it's easy to make a list of the things that you want in a lease or any other agreement. One does not always get everything one wants in life. You will not get all of the lease provisions that you would like. Arranging a lease or license agreement involves negotiation, and negotiation, of course, means giving and taking. If you are negotiating with one of the theatres considered to be a more desirable house, then you will be bargaining from weakness, as these theatres are much in demand. Even though you can't always have everything you want in the lease, it should be helpful to know what you ought to want and to know what you are giving up.

Variety of Theatres

The variety of theatres that one may choose from off-Broadway in New York City is great. There are proscenium theatres, theatres-in-the-round, three-quarters in the round, and some cabarets which have been converted to theatres. Almost all of the off-Broadway houses today have adequate heat in the winter time and adequate air conditioning during the summer. There was a time not so long ago when the off-Broadway theatres lacked the comforts that most theatregoers have learned to expect.

6 Cast, Crew and Personnel

The theatre you select is extremely important. The property you select is terribly important. The selection of the people who will be working in and on the show is also vitally important. I can't and won't say that any one thing or person is more important than any other. Everyone knows for sure that raising the money is important, for without the money you would not be selecting a property, a theatre, or personnel. I have participated in discussions into the wee hours of the night as to whether the director is more important than the star, or whether the stage manager is more important than the set designer. This is utter nonsense. They are all critically important and it behooves you to select all wisely for therein may lie the difference between a flop and a smash hit.

The Director

Hopefully by the time you obtain the property, you will have given some serious thought to whom you would like to direct the play. In fact, right after you acquire the property, as soon as you can, you should find yourself a director. Very often there is a great deal of pre-production work for the director to do and it is sometimes necessary that the play be rewritten. The director is the natural person to work with the playwright to supervise and assist with the rewriting if it is required. If there is no necessity for rewriting immediately after you acquire the property, relax and rest assured that by the time the curtain goes up on opening night there will have been some changes in the script. Chances are that the director will assist you not only in working with the author on rewrites, but will also help you raise the money by staging backers' auditions if you need them.

Just as you are the chief with respect to the entire show, and especially with the running of the business end of the show, you should select a director in whom you have confidence so that he can be in charge of what happens on stage artistically. Actually, he works for you and if you're not happy with what he is doing, you can, of course, (and your agreement should provide that you can) replace him. However, you should never lose sight of the fact that you are the producer and not the director. If you want to direct the show do so, but don't do it until you have had an opportunity to read further on about conflicts of interest and other problems that may arise when a producer directs his own show.

Having decided on the director you want, and having discussed with him in great detail all of the artistic aspects of the play, you then must hire him. The terms of the agreement you enter into with the director will depend upon his experience and how badly you want him; it will depend upon whether you are bargaining from strength or from weakness. The Society of Stage Directors and Choreographers has an off-Broadway Minimum Basic Contract. Although not all of the producers have signed with them, many of the directors have. If you wish to use a director who is a member of the union, then you must give him at least the minimum provided for in this agreement. Actually most directors, except very new directors, will receive near the Society minimum anyhow without the union requirements to support them.

The Society of Stage Directors and Choreographers Minimum Basic Contract provides that the minimum fee for a director shall be no less than $500, 50% to be paid to the director on signing of the contract, 25% to be paid on the first day of rehearsal, and 25% on the first day of the third week of rehearsal. All of these payments are a fee and deemed non-returnable, but not advances against the royalty payments.

In addition to the basic fee, the director shall be paid a minimum guaranteed royalty payment in the amount of $25 if the gross weekly box-office receipts are $2500 or less, $30 if the gross weekly box-office receipts are more than $2500 but less than $3000, $40 if the gross weekly box-office receipts are more than $3000 but less than $3500, $50 if the gross weekly box-office receipts are more than $3500 but less than $4000, $75 if the gross weekly box-office receipts are more than $4000 but less than $5000, and 2% of the gross weekly box-office receipts in excess of $5000. Gross weekly box-office receipts are specifically defined in the agreement.

The agreement also provides that the director shall have the option to direct all other productions of the show at the above stated minimum fee. There is provision for the director receiving billing credit on a separate line in a size of type and position as agreed upon. The director shall have cast, understudy, replacement, set designer, costume designer, and stage manager approval which he will not unreasonably withhold. The director must have two house seats reserved for him except when there are theatre parties. The director agrees that he will supervise and maintain the quality of the production.

Apart from the Society minimum, director's fees usually range from between $500 and $900. I know there are some directors who will get $1000 or maybe even more, but it is most unusual, just as it's most unusual for a director to get a fee of $150. The royalty payments usually range between 1% and 2½% of the gross weekly box-office receipts.

Billing credits are always a problem. Like the author, the director will often ill-advisedly insist that his name be the largest name on the program, in the ad, or wherever billing credits are given. This may prevent the producer from getting a star that would be most desirable for the part.

A provision that the director may have the option to direct future productions is all right so long as it is confined solely to future productions over which this producer has some control, and the agreement must so provide.

The Stage Manager

Selection of a good stage manager is a most important job. Prior to and after opening, the stage manager is responsible for coordination of everything that happens backstage, including the proper lighting as designed by the lighting designer, any recordings which must be played, all off-stage noises, and slide projection or film strips if required. The stage manager is exactly what the name implies, that is, he is the manager of the stage. As such manager, he is in charge of all things on the stage as well as all people on the stage. The importance of the stage manager cannot possibly be over emphasized.

All script changes must go through the stage manager for he is responsible for light cues, sound cues, actors' cues, and is, in addition to all this, the director's right hand. It is his duty to make certain that the sets are changed properly, that the props are all where they should be, that the actors and actresses make their entrances on time, and that everything is coordinated. All of the backstage detail and leg work which must be done is handled by or supervised by the stage manager; sometimes after instructions from the director, but sometimes on his own initiative.

After the show has opened, in the absence of the director, the stage manager assumes the role of the director, that is, he may call rehearsals, do replacement casting, and direct the rehearsals. The stage manager's job starts before rehearsals commence and ends a few weeks after the show closes. During the time that he is working, he is very busy.

The Cast

The cast is selected by the director with the assistance of the

producer and the approval of the author. The stage manager assists
with the auditions and very often contributes his advice. The job
basically ought to be the director's and although you as the producer
will be hiring the cast and should be satisfied, unless you have strong
objections to anyone you ought to give the director a good deal of
leeway to exercise his judgment You should have selected a director
you have faith in and trust, and this being a very important part of
his job is part of the reason that you hired him. Just make certain
that your motivation as well as the director's for casting a particular
person is consistent with what is in the best interest of the play. Hiring
with the help of a casting couch is not recommended.

The Actors' Equity Association Contract

The Actors' Equity Association Off-Broadway Contract expired
on October 31, 1967, and since the League of Off-Broadway Theatres
did not reach agreement with Equity on a new contract, the old contract was extended until November 26, 1967. A new contract was
negotiated which became effective as of November 13, 1967, which
incorporated some significant changes.

The minimum off-Broadway payment to an Equity actor increases
in amount, depending upon the gross weekly box-office receipts, and
the minimum is further increased at the end of each year. The figures
are as follows:

Box-Office Receipts Weekly Gross	During First Year Ending Nov. 3, 1968	During Second Year Ending Nov. 2, 1969	During Third Year Ending Nov. 1, 1970
Under $4500	$ 70.00	$ 72.50	$ 75.00
$4500 to $5500	75.00	77.50	80.00
$5500 to $6500	85.00	87.50	90.00
$6500 to $7500	95.00	97.50	100.00
$7500 to $8500	110.00	112.50	115.00
$8500 to $9000	130.00	132.50	135.00
$9000 to $9500	137.50	142.50	145.00
Over $9500	145.00	147.50	150.00

In addition to the salary payments, a payment is made in the amount
of $3.25 per week per Equity personnel for hospital and welfare bene-

fits and a payment of 2% of the gross weekly box-office receipts or 2% of the payroll, whichever is higher, to the Equity pension fund.

The minimum payable to a stage manager is $20 above the applicable minimum payable to an actor. An assistant stage manager is not required, however, if one is employed, then he is to be paid $10 above the applicable minimum payable to an actor. An assistant stage manager may also act and understudy parts in the play. A dance captain is not required, however, if you do use a dance captain he must be paid $10 above the applicable minimum payable to an actor.

An actor who has completed forty-four (44) weeks of non-consecutive employment in a show which grosses below $8500 per week, will be paid an additional $7.50 per week. This was intended to compensate actors in long-running productions in small houses where they could not take advantage of the pay raises which occur as the gross box-office receipts increase.

The maximum weekly rehearsal time for shows after opening was reduced from ten hours to eight hours, and no rehearsal is permitted on days when a show has two performances.

It is now possible to sign an actor to a limited run-of-the-play contract, or up to nine months, whichever is shorter, providing that the actor is paid a minimum of $150 each week. Unless an actor is signed to a run-of-the-play contract or up to nine months, the actor may leave the production upon two weeks notice. The producer, likewise, may terminate the actor's employment upon two weeks notice.

In spite of the Equity minimum there are occasions when you will pay a particular star as much as $750 per week. What's more, such an extravagance might be money well spent. Almost always however, the cast is hired for the Equity minimum and their greater remuneration comes from the opportunity to work and the exposure that it brings.

Sets, Costumes, and Lights

You will also have to make some contractual arrangements with your set designer, costume designer, and lighting designer. In some instances, the sets, costumes, and lights are all done by one person, and in other instances you may use two or three people. In all events the set designer very often creates the designs and is responsible for the execution and construction of the sets.

The United Scenic Artists Minimum Basic Contract provides that in a theatre with between 250 and 299 seats, the minimum payable to the set designer is for five days at the rate of $40.81 per day, the $204.05 payable to the Union at the time of contract signing. After the fifth week, that is beginning with the sixth week, the set designer is to be paid a royalty of $40.81 per week during the run of the show.

The United Scenic Artists Minimum Basic Contract for a theatre of between 200 and 250 seats is in the amount of $40.81 per day for a at least four days, the $163.24 payable to the Union at the time of contract signing. The royalty payment which commences beginning with the sixth week is in the amount of $32.64 per week during the run of the show.

The United Scenic Artists Minimum Basic Contract for a theatre under 200 seats provides that the set designer will be paid the sum of $40.81 for a minimum of three days, the $122.43 payable to the Union at the time of contract signing. At the commencement of the sixth week the designer will be paid a royalty of $24.48 per week during the run of the show. The set designer will most likely be paid a fee ranging between the Union minimum and $750.00.

Like the set designer, the costume designer, off-Broadway, very often not only designs the costumes but actually physically makes them. The United Scenic Artists Minimum payable to a costume designer is at the rate of $35 per day for not less than one day, payable at contract signing. The costume designer will usually be paid a fee ranging between $150 and $500 for the costumes, and may be reimbursed for the cost of materials.

The United Scenic Artists does not at the present time have a separate contract covering the lighting design, and the minimums payable for the lighting designer are the same as the minimums payable to the scenic designer which are set forth above.

Press Agent

Your press agent will handle all the press releases for the show, will arrange for television and radio interviews for the stars and other members of the cast and crew, and will do everything possible to keep the name of the show and its principals in the public eye. It's a very important job. As later noted, if you are in a theatre over 200 you must have an ATPAM press agent and company manager, and if you are in a theatre under 200, one or the other must belong to ATPAM. In the smaller house you will probably choose to have the press agent as an ATPAM member rather than the company manager.

If the press agent you select is a member of ATPAM, his minimum fee for an off-Broadway show will depend upon the number of seats in the theatre. If it is less than 149 seats his minimum fee will be $150, if less than 199 seats, $165, if less than 299 seats $175, if less than 499 seats $200 and if over 499 seats at the Broadway scale which is $350 until September 1, 1970, $360 until September 1, 1971 and $375 until September 1, 1972.

Advertising Agency

The press agent should be distinguished from the advertising agency. The advertising agency will handle the paid newspapers ads and other paid advertisements. The press agent is responsible for all of the publicity but especially the publicity that is not paid for. The press agent will, of course, also assist the planning and execution of the paid advertising. Actually the paid ads are usually prepared by the advertising agency after consultation between the producer, the press agent, and the general manager. There are a couple of advertising agencies in the City of New York which specialize in theatrical advertising, and they handle almost all of the theatrical advertising.

General Manager

Your production may have a general manager, a company manager, or both. If you are in an off-Broadway theatre with under 200 seats, you must have a member of the Association of Theatrical Press Agents and Managers, commonly referred to as ATPAM, as either your press agent or your manager. If you are in an off-Broadway theater with over 200 seats, then you must have both an ATPAM press agent and an ATPAM company manager.

The general manager will negotiate (in conjunction with the attorney), administer, and supervise the practical and financial procedures on behalf of the company, including all banking transactions. He will obtain, contact, and hire all required non-artistic theatre and production personnel that may become necessary, and if requested by the producer may also participate in the negotiation of contracts for the artistic personnel. He will, as I've pointed out, prepare the production and operating budgets. He will have the over-all responsibility of the payment of all company bills from the company accounts, as well as the preparation and filing of all tax returns on time. He may negotiate for the rental of the theatre. He will supervise the sale of all tickets and box-office procedures and in conjunction with the company's accounting firm he should render to the producer a weekly profit and loss statement of the company's operation, including an itemized accounting of all production expenditures. A good general manager is invaluable to an Off-Broadway production, especially when the producer himself lacks experience. The producer is, of course, responsible for the ultimate decisions of the producing company, however, a good general manager will make it easier for the producer to make those decisions and will help put the decisions into effect.

Company Manager

The duties of a general manager and a company manager may overlap, and there is sometimes not a clear delineation between the two jobs. Perhaps the most significant distinction is that the general manager's job is concerned with policy making and the company manager's job is on a non-policy making level. The company manager attends to the actors' non-personal needs and is concerned with the day to day operation of the show on a business basis. ATPAM requires that the company manager be hired one week prior to the first paid performance, and the general manager will have been doing his job for many weeks before this. The company manager must be at the theatre each night to check the box-office receipts, to count the house, to check the tickets, and to conduct whatever business is required at each performance.

The general manager, who is a member of ATPAM, may be his own company manager; however, there are occasions when a general manager will employ another person to handle the chore of being company manager. The minimum for an ATPAM company manager is $165.40 per week and a two week bond must be deposited. There are also payments required for vacation (4% of the salary), pension (1% of the salary), and an amount for hospitalization and welfare.

Accountants and Accountings

The New York Theatrical Financing Act enacted in 1964, which is part of the General Business Law of the State of New York, provides that every theatrical producer must within four months after the end of each twelve month period (beginning with the first expenditure of investors' funds) or within four months after the last public performance of the original production in the state, whichever first occurs, furnish to all investors and to the Department of Law of the State of New York a written balance sheet and statement of profit and loss prepared by an independent public accountant with an opinion by the accountant that these statements fairly present the financial position and results of operations of the production company. Each of these statements must be a "certified statement."

In addition, a producer must furnish each investor and the Department of Law of the State of New York with an accurate and truthful itemized statement of income and expenditures for every six month period not covered by a previously issued certified statement which must be subscribed to by the producer as accurate, and must be furnished within three months after the close of such six month period. After the last public performance in the state of the original production, the producer must report to the investors and to the Department of Law within four months after the end of each year thereafter with respect to subsequent earnings or expenditures by the production, which report must be subscribed by the producer as accurate.

The Department of Law of the State of New York is authorized to issue an exemption from furnishing certified statements if the offering is for less than $75,000 or if the offering is made to less than 26 persons. This will of course be available to all off-Broadway shows because it is unlikely that the budget will exceed $75,000.00.

In order to take advantage of this exemption, it is necessary that your attorney file a form known as an "Application for Exemption from Accounting Requirements — Article 26 — A." This statement sets forth the fact that you are producing a play and that the total capitalization is in a specified amount and the number of persons to whom the offering has been made. The application will also state that the producer will see that the statements above set forth are prepared; however, they need not be certified statements. With each statement there must be a letter of transmittal which states that it constitutes a true, accurate, and complete reflection of the financial transactions of the production.

It is advisable that you select an accountant familiar with theatre, as the business problems of a theatrical production are somewhat unique. There are competent theatrical accountants in the City of New York who are conscious of all those peculiar problems that one may expect to encounter in an off-Broadway show.

Attorney

Hire a good theatrical attorney who knows the business. If he knows the business, you can rely on him to perform the kind of legal services you should have, and in addition he will assist you with all kinds of advice which you as a producer will find helpful. If he knows the business, he won't charge you too much for he will know that an off-Broadway budget cannot compensate him for all the work he will do.

7　Musicals

Off-Broadway musicals have some additional items and additional personnel to consider. Musicals are of course more expensive to produce because arrangements are needed, musicians are needed, a choreographer and arranger must be hired. The consideration of selection of a theatre is different and of course casting is different. The actors must not only act well but must sing and move well. The original cast album can be very important to a musical.

A musical show may have an original story, may be an adaptation of a previously published novel or a previously published straight play, may be a revival, or may be a musical revue. At the present time it is almost impossible to make it with a revue in a theatre as the theatregoing public during the past 25 years has been revued to death.

Off-Broadway revivals of shows previously produced on Broadway have currently been in vogue. The problem with such a revival is that most Broadway musicals have large casts and often in the transfer to off-Broadway the show is not trimmed enough to sustain the play in such a small theatre with off-Broadway ticket prices. Furthermore, what were successful Broadway productions of some years ago cannot withstand the scaling down to the off-Broadway level because the book was so flimsy in the first place. Musical theatre has undergone a development and evolution and the story in a musical of today has an importance that it did not have in the musicals of former years.

I have on many occasions spoken with producer clients and writer clients who are overwhelmed with the music for a particular play and, in fact, they are so overwhelmed that they cannot understand how the play can be anything but a smash hit with such music. "Just wait till you hear the music," is a common plea. What every producer doing a musical must always bear in mind is, how is the book? It's rare that a musical in today's theatre is successful without a good book. In fact many professional producers will not waste their time listening to the score of a musical until they have had a chance to read the script. If the script isn't strong, they feel that the music can't make any difference. Bear this in mind when you select a musical play for production. Excellent music will rarely make up for an almost good script.

Original Cast Album

Usually the option agreement with the author, composer, and lyricist, will provide that the receipts from the original cast album shall be shared with the author, composer, and lyricist receiving 60% of the net receipts and the producer receiving 40% of the net receipts. An original cast album differs from other subsidiary rights in that not only does the author, composer, and lyricist enter into the agreement, but the producer who controls the cast must also make the deal with the record company. The contract is often between the recording company and the producer with the author, composer, and lyricist approving the contract, usually through their publishing company.

Usually the play must run for at least 21 performances before a recording company is obligated to make an original cast album. The contract will provide that the producer must furnish the cast, the members of the orchestra, and the conductor. The cast and musicians are actually paid by the recording company for their services; however, these payments will constitute an advance chargeable against the royalty payments paid to the author, composer, lyricist, and producer. In addition the recording company will furnish the studio and all equipment. The producer has to furnish copies of the orchestrations and arrangements of the musical compositions.

Most often the agreement will provide that the recording company has an exclusive on an original cast album for a period of five years, and the performers are restricted for five years from performing for any other record company what they do on the original cast album. The royalty payable by the recording company to the author, composer, lyricist (it varies how they share this payment), and the producer, is usually between five and ten percent of the suggested list retail price, or between ten and twenty percent of the wholesale price. Royalties are almost always paid on ninety percent of the records sold. There are very often provisions in the contract that the company need not pay royalties on free records, and will pay a very much reduced royalty on records distributed through record clubs. One must be careful to limit in some fashion the number of free records and the distribution through record clubs at the reduced royalty, as it is possible for the record company to use your particular record as the advertising bait to sell other records.

Also bear in mind that the royalty payment is based on the replacement cost of the record (this is so whether it be based on a percentage of the wholesale or retail price) which means that they do do not pay a royalty on the cost of the album cover, jacket, or box. Sometimes the cost of the album cover, jacket, or box is left for later determination. Sometimes the agreement fixes it in a given amount, and sometimes the agreement will provide that ten percent of the wholesale price of the record shall be deemed to be the cost of the cover. The contracts usually provide for billing credits to the recording company in all advertising, house seats for the recording company, an arbitration clause, and so on.

Of course this is the barest outline of a contract for an original cast album, as there are many other important provisions in such an agreement. Even the terms that are herein mentioned are most negoti-able, that is, they may vary in either direction from what is set forth above.

Publisher

The publisher of the composer and lyricist is usually the one who arranges the original cast album, in exchange for which the publisher shares the composer-lyricist's receipts from the album. When one thinks of a publisher, one usually thinks of publishing, that is printing sheet music. This can be part of the job of a publisher, however, printing has become relatively less important. Most publishers are anxious to sign up a new composer and lyricist that they consider talented, not for the right to print the sheet music which they write, but mostly because of the income that can flow from recordings, the manufacture of recordings, and the performance of recordings.

Musicians

All musicals running which have established contracts with the musicians can continue the existing arrangement. However, the American Federation of Musicians, Local 802, wants to negotiate each new show separately and individually. The union takes the position that the musicians fees will vary depending upon the location of the theatre, the size of the theatre, the ticket price range, the total budget of the show, and other considerations. There being no standard contract, since each deal is different, you had best get some indication from your General Manager as to what you may expect either from his past experience, or from his making a trip to the union office.

Arrangements

When a composer finishes composing the music for a show, he has a lead sheet or at most an arrangement for the piano. Most off-Broad-way musicals have between two and five musicians and the music must be arranged for the various instruments which will be used. It goes without saying that you should not be extravagant with the number of musicians, as an off-Broadway show cannot afford the luxury of a full pit orchestra. Some musicians double on one or more instruments. Many sax players can handle a clarinet and this can mean dollar savings to you.

When a decision has been made as to the instruments which will be used, you will need an arranger to arrange the music for those instruments. Do not forget that as the producer, the decision on the number of instruments is yours to make. Bear in mind that the composer and the director will be of invaluable service in assisting with this decision, but paying the bills is your job and not theirs. Use discretion consistent with your limited budget.

The musical arranger will usually be paid a fee ranging between $500 and $750. Sometimes the composer may wish to do the arrangements, but if not don't be disappointed. Get a good arranger who has rapport with the composer and understands the play.

On Broadway a special dance arranger will be hired. Off-Broadway, the arranger usually handles the dance numbers as well as the vocal numbers.

Choreographer

The director may wish to and may be qualified to handle the choreography. If not you will need a choreographer. The choreographer will be paid between $250 and $500 as a fee, the amount depending on how much dancing is in the show and how well-known the choreographer is.

If the choreographer is a member of the Society of Stage Directors and Choreographers, then the minimum basic terms of their agreement will be applicable. Their minimum basic fee for a choreographer is $375 with fifty (50%) percent being paid upon the signing of the contract, twenty-five (25%) percent being paid on the first day of rehearsal, and twenty-five (25%) percent being paid on the first day of the third week of rehearsal. In addition, the agreement provides for a minimum guaranteed royalty payment of $25 on the gross weekly box-office receipts up to $2500, $30 if the gross weekly box-office receipts are in excess of $2500 but less than $3000, $40 if the gross weekly box-office receipts are in excess of $3000 but less than $4000, $50 if the gross weekly box-office receipts are in excess of $4000 but less than $5000, and 1½% of the gross weekly box-office receipts in excess of $5000. There is also a provision that the choreographer shall have an option to do the choreography for all other productions at the above stated minimum fee. This of course should be limited to productions under control of the producer. The choreographer is also granted approval of the rehearsal pianist and there are, of course, provisions for his billing credits as well as a provision for house seats.

Musical Director

The musical director is the conductor. He plays one of the instruments, almost always the piano. He is paid, as we noted, an amount as negotiated with the union. On occasions the composer may insist on being the musical director. If there is a choreographer the musical director will advise him.

8   Rehearsals, Open, Run or Close

Selection of a date for opening the show can be extremely important. Of course, the date for the commencement of rehearsals will be dependent upon the date selected for the opening. If possible you should make every effort to open the show on a night when there is nothing else opening. Your opening night date may be registered with the League of Off-Broadway Theatres, and the first show registered for a particular date would have priority as far as press coverage is concerned. It sometimes happens that a Broadway show is scheduled to open on the same date on which an off-Broadway show is scheduled. Under such circumstances even though the Broadway show may have later decided on that date, the first string critics would give priority to the Broadway show so it becomes necessary to change the off-Broadway opening date.

There are certain times during the year that theatre business is better than other times. I've previously mentioned that it is not advisable to open a show between the beginning of May and the end of August. You should also bear in mind that the first three weeks in December are death for theatre; however, they are followed by the holiday week between Christmas and New Year which is a great theatre business week. Immediately after New Year, there is again a slack period for several weeks. Religious holidays are generally slow nights. Weekends of course are busier than weekdays. All of this should be carefully considered so that you will have sufficient funds to withstand the rough periods if your show is doing marginal business.

Rehearsals

You will want to plan on at least three weeks of rehearsals; four weeks is most co.nmon. As a producer you should welcome the cast and staff at the first rehearsal. After the first rehearsal, you should make yourself somewhat scarce and should not interfere with the director's job. By this I mean that you should not spend every day during every rehearsal hour in the theatre with the director. It is important that you show your face backstage on occasions so that the cast and crew know you are interested in them and in the show. Of course you should also follow the progress of the show so that if the director is in trouble you may assist or replace him. This can be done without your constant presence in the theatre during rehearsals.

As the producer you will have many other important things to do during rehearsal periods as there is a great deal of work which should be done in connection with the promotion of the play. During this period you must complete the plans for your advertising campaign, arrange theatre parties, and set up every promotion device that you can conceive of. There will be tickets to order, programs to set up and get printed, posters to distribute. Your general manager will assist with these items. It is necessary to follow the progress of the play carefully. There will be rewriting sessions with the author which you will want to attend. There will be personality problems with the cast that you will have to attend to. There will be hands to hold and tempers to cool. You will start losing all objectivity during this period if you are not careful, that is if you still have any left.

Previews

Most off-Broadway productions will preview for between seven and fourteen performances. To preview simply means that the show plays for paid audiences prior to the opening at a reduced ticket price. Previews serve the same purpose as out-of-town tryouts do for a Broadway show, to give the director, the cast and all involved in the production an opportunity to see the audience reaction. Changes will be incorporated based on the audience response. Even some Broadway shows have now abandoned the idea of out-of-town try-outs and use only previews. It sometimes happens that some shows do better business during previews than they do after the reviews are published. This has led to the comment that "That show should have continued previewing and never should have opened."

During previews, producers will sometimes paper the house. The term "paper" is a name for free tickets. It may come as a surprise to you that everyone in the business usually pays for their tickets. The exceptions arise during previews or if the show is in trouble after opening. In both instances an audience is desirable. A producer will generally call Actors' Equity and the USO to tell them that they may send some people to see the show, or everyone in the cast and crew will be asked to call their friends and relatives to attend. In all events, it is terribly important that there be people watching the show as an empty house can destroy the cast's morale. Papering for this reason should always be considered and used with discretion.

Opening Night

On opening night there is unbelievable excitement and much nervous tension in the air. Most shows open at 7:30 P.M. as the newspapers must make their deadline. The tickets may read 7:00 P.M. but it's usually 7:15 or 7:30 P.M. when the curtain goes up. You must make sure that it doesn't go up much later than 7:30 P.M., as you are certain to antagonize those reviewers who do have a deadline to make.

Reviews

The importance of reviews has not changed much in the last few years; however, the number of reviews in the City of New York by daily newspapers has markedly changed. At the present writing the important dailies are the New York Times, the New York Post, and the Daily News. Of course there are a host of other reviews that can be important such as The Saturday Review, Cue Magazine, The New Yorker, Variety, The Morning Telegraph, The Village Voice, The Villager, and Women's Wear Daily (these are not necessarily in order of importance), however, it is pretty well believed that unless one has a good review from the New York Times and at least one other daily, it's most difficult to try to run the show. The television reviews are becoming increasingly important, but we cannot minimize the extreme importance of the New York Times. I think that a New York Times rave review by itself might be enough without any of the other major reviews, however, it's most unlikely that a play which gets a good New York Times review won't get at least one other good review somewhere else.

Party

After the opening night performance, it is not uncommon for the producer or for the producing company to throw a cast party. It's usually labelled a "cast party," but the persons invited will include, in addition to the cast and crew, friends of the production and may sometimes include investors. The location of the party may vary from someone's home (it should be large as you may rest assured that the cast and everyone else that's invited will not feel bashful about bringing guests with them) to a restaurant or hotel. I have attended off-Broadway opening parties at some of the most exclusive restaurants in the City of New York including VOISIN, SARDI'S, THE PENTHOUSE, and LA COMEDIE. Unfortunately, the degree of elegance of the party doesn't always reflect the condition of what happened on the stage. Some of the nicest parties sometimes follow some of the most disappointing productions and vice versa. In all events, if the reviews are not good, the party will soon be over. The television reviews start coming around 11:00 P. M. and there may be three or less. The New York Times is out about 12:30 A.M., but usually the press agent gets the review around midnight from someone at the Times.

After Opening Night

After opening night, as the producer, you may be faced with a very serious decision, that is, whether or not you should close the show or attempt to run it. If the reviews are all bad, or mostly all bad, then your decision, although a heartbreaking one, is an easy one to make. You simply close the show as soon as possible. It will be difficult but you should accept the facts of life. If you have rave reviews in all of the dailies, again your decision is a relatively easy one. You've got to keep the show alive until the public starts buying tickets in large quantities, and you find yourself the producer of a sold-out show. With such reviews, this is not too difficult to contemplate.

The difficult decision comes when you have one good review from the three dailies and some television support, or some support from the weekly or monthly publications. Any situation which is less than all raves, where you figure that between 50% and 70% of the reviews are good, presents a situation which requires a most difficult business decision. It's even difficult if you can be somewhat objective in making the decision which, of course, at this point is a total impossibility. Your objectivity at this particular moment may be rated as zero.

If you close the show immediately you may be in a position to return to the backers some money that will be left after paying off all of the obligations. Returning any money to backers is good public relations and you will be needing backers for later shows, that is if you don't decide to cut your wrists. If you decide to run the show, you may obligate yourself for amounts in excess of the budget. It means that you, as the producer, the general partner, will have to reach into your pocket for the cash, as you are personally responsible for all sums spent in excess of the capitalization of the partnership. There may be some rich investors in the show who will help by making loans to the company which are returnable only from partnership profits, in an attempt to see that the play is kept alive until it has a reasonable chance for the word of mouth to start carrying the show. What's important is that a decision be made which has some basis in reality. It doesn't make too much difference whether you throw out your money or you throw out an investor's money, if in fact the money should not have been thrown out in the first place.

It is not unusual for a producer to request that persons receiving weekly royalties waive that royalty during losing weeks after opening, if money is needed to keep the show alive. It is to the interest of everyone involved in the production that it get a long run, and such a request is not unreasonable provided that at the same time, the producer waives his producer's fee and, under some circumstances, even the cash office charge.

After the opening and the reviews are in, it's customary the following day to meet in the office of the advertising agency to try and put an ad together. It is the popular consensus that very little money should be spent for advertising on an off-Broadway show prior to its opening. After the opening the reviews are carefully screened for "quotes," and this is the time to spend the money. You can figure on your advertising bill running between $750 and $1500 per week at this time, as compared to between $500 and $750 during a normal operating week. You should think of larger sums being spent immediately after the opening and tapering off the amount spent as the play picks up momentum.

It is permissible, without receiving permission, to quote an entire review or part of a review, as long as you do not select bits and pieces in such a manner as to misrepresent what was said. You cannot quote, "A pretty awful play, and the parts were not well acted," as "A pretty ... play ... well acted." If you do try to distort the meaning, the newspapers most of the time will not accept your ad, so it is not easy for you to get yourself into trouble in this fashion even if you want to.

It is at this meeting at the ad agency that the very basic question, to close or to try for a run, must first be faced. A decision of course can be postponed, but if it looks like the chances of success are marginal, then the decision ought not to be unreasonably delayed. At the meeting the general manager, the company manager, the press agent, the advertising agent, the attorney, the accountant, and any other interested parties will attempt to counsel you. Please do not be upset if your general manager, your accountant, your attorney, or other interested parties who have had much theatre experience, try to save you heartache, wear and tear, and money by recommending that you close the show. This does not mean that the persons making this recommendation like the show any less than they did before it opened, nor does it mean that they like the show any less than you do. It just means that they may have a more objective attitude about the possibility of making a successful run of the show; they want to do the merciful thing and save you as much time, energy and money as can be saved with as little hurt as possible.

I've seen it happen on so many occasions that a general manager or one of the other interested parties, in all good conscience, recommends that a show close and the producer, because of his fiery zeal, total involvement, lack of sleep and over-consumption of scotch, accuses the well-intentioned manager of not having faith in the show and being a quitter. This well-intentioned, totally correct, well-motivated person, giving such advice will, of course, later be blamed by the producer for having been responsible for the failure of the show, simply because he wisely advised that the show should be closed.

The decision to close the show, of course, in its final analysis is the producer's, and it's a terribly important decision. In making the decision please understand the motivation of the people around you. Know that they are trying to help you, to do what they can to assist you, and that this help should not be misunderstood to be traitorous or not in your best interests.

Scaling the House, Twofers, and Discount Tickets

It may be very important to you how the house is scaled, which means what the ticket prices are. An off-Broadway musical customarily charges more than an off-Broadway dramatic or comedy show. As you know, prices are higher on weekends. Your general manager will assist you in pricing the tickets so that you receive a maximum return on ticket sales and at the same time maintain attractive competitive prices.

"Twofers" are printed tickets which are distributed which can be exchanged at the box-office for two tickets for the price of one. These are printed and distributed throughout the city at hotels, schools, and other places of public assembly.

You may also purchase the use of a carefully selected list of 6500 people which includes English teachers, drama teachers, speech teachers, literature and history teachers, principals and educators of colleges, high schools, junior high schools, and parochial schools, within a 125 mile radius of New York City. Such a mailing can be particularly useful if the play is the kind of play that would have appeal to students. The returns from this mailing list have proven very successful.

Twofers and student discount tickets would likely be used either at the beginning of a run or near the end of a run. Such tickets would be desirable at the inception if the show has a chance of running and it is necessary to stay alive for a few weeks until the tickets start selling. If your show didn't get decent reviews, don't think that twofers or student discount tickets can save the show. They may be very helpful in bridging a gap, but cannot alone make a financially successful show out of a flop. After the show has run for some length of time and business begins to fall off, you may also want to consider the use of twofers and student discount tickets.

9 Repertories, Children's Theatre, Off-Off and Resident Professional Theatre

Repertory Company

Every now and then someone gets the idea that there should be an off-Broadway repertory company and proceeds to try and organize such a company, usually with a particular kind of theatre in mind. Of course, there is the theatre-in-the-park where productions of Shakespeare are presented, which is geographically not Broadway, but technically is not an off-Broadway theatre since it seats over 300 persons. This is a completely different kind of an operation than most off-Broadway producers will be engaged in since it receives grants and is not self-sustaining.

I have, on occasions, been confronted by a client who wants to set up a repertory theatre based on a particular country, a particular author, or a particular kind of show; for example, suspense thrillers. If you want to organize a repertory company, that is, to do more than one show with the same actors, you had best finance the production in such a way that you have enough money to do three or four shows before you start, without expecting any remuneration from the first or second production. What very often happens is that a producer raises enough money to do more than one show but less than two shows and feels that there is no danger of not having enough money to do the second show, the third show, and then the fourth show, because the first, second, and third ones will be successful. What sometimes happens is that the wrong one or wrong two of the four plays are first chosen (maybe all four are wrong) and after the first show opens and doesn't make enough money to finance the second one, he is then out of business.

I've discovered from my clients' experience that it is usually easier to raise money for four separate shows one at a time than it is to raise enough money in the first instance to do four shows, one after the other. Someone will always find a reason why they like one show or two shows but not all of them. Most people are not really anxious to get involved in a producing company that will go on producing indefinitely, keeping all the money that it earns to do more shows rather than returning the money to the investors. Even if the company makes money on the first or second show, if a repertory company runs long enough, it will continue to produce shows until it eventually runs out of money. It is highly unlikely that the company can continually come in with successes, and by the law of averages the money must eventually run out.

With one show the investors know that after the reserve is raised, all of the net profits will be paid to them. With a repertory company the investors know that after the first show the profits will be kept for the next show. Even where the partnership is formed for the production of one single play, the limited partnership agreement as we earlier learned, may provide that the profits may be used for additional productions of this particular play, so it is possible that the investors will be investing their money in future productions of the same play. At least the investors know what they are getting into when they invest in a single play, and know that they are fastening their faith to this single known play.

Children's Theatre

Most usually the groups that produce Children's Theatre are repertory companies; the same actors and actresses present different children's plays. Some of the Children's Theatre that I represent is not just attractive to children but has remarkable appeal for adults.

If you are contemplating producing Children's Theatre, you should be aware of the fact that there are serious business problems which are very nearly insurmountable. The artistic problems are solvable, that is, reasonable compromises can be made. Most of the children's shows are presented on Saturday morning in a theatre which already has another production in it. As a result it is often necessary to improvise easily movable sets and props and to present the show on a stage already filled with the sets that are there for the show that is presently occupying the theatre. The lights are all focussed for the show that is in the theatre and cannot be changed. This kind of an adjustment may be slightly incovenient but can easily be made.

The business problems with the production of Children's Theatre can readily be seen when one realizes that the shows play to a relatively poor market. Children cannot afford to pay and their parents won't pay what is charged for tickets to an adult show. A Children's Theatre production will usually charge $1.00 or at most $1.50 per seat. If you're in an off-Broadway theatre and you have 199 seats or even 299 seats, you can see immediately that your gross box-office receipts are going to be very limited. Figure that you are going to pay the cast of between 9 and 16 actors $10 or $15 per performance. Add theatre rental, and if you're lucky it will be no more than $100 per day. You must pay the needed box-office help, ushers, stage manager, and so on, and it's easy to see that the chance of making money from off-Broadway Children's Theatre is possible but not probable. You would have to cut corners and fill, or nearly fill, the theatre for every performance, or be heavily endowed.

There are many theatres outside the City of New York that will seat 600, 800, or 1000 children, and even larger tents which offer a potential for the presentation of Children's Theatre. The problem is to make certain that there are enough bookings in such places to pay for all of the expenses incidental to running a going business.

Off-Off-Broadway

One must not overlook the contribution that has been made to theatre by what is known as the off-off-Broadway theatres. The off-off-Broadway theatres, if they are functioning with Equity actors, present shows either as a showcase or as a workshop production. There are specific regulations promulgated by Actors' Equity Association setting forth the requirements of a showcase presentation and a workshop presentation, and members of Actors' Equity are forbidden to work in a production unless there is a strict compliance with the rules as established by Equity. The reason, of course, is to make certain that actors are not exploited.

What very often happens, and everyone in the business knows that it's happening, is that an off-off-Broadway producer purports to have a non-Equity production and does not comply with the Equity regulations. Oftentimes Equity actors who are unemployed are so anxious to be working that they will appear in an off-off-Broadway non-Equity production under an assumed name. This kind of dishonesty is also not recommended. There's no good reason why a producer ought to jeopardize the career of an actor by asking that actor to do something contrary to the regulations of his association. Either present a non-Equity production or abide by the rules of Actors' Equity Association. It means less headaches, and if you are going to be in the business it's desirable that you establish yourself as one who is responsible and honest.

At the time this is being written there are, in Manhattan alone, over one hundred and twenty-five off-off-Broadway theatres in existence. Sixty-five of these theatres are members of the Off-Off-Broadway Alliance, a cooperative organization which was established to promote recognition for off-off-Broadway as a significant cultural force and to help its member theatres achieve their artistic goals.

At any particular time it is possible to see a variety of different presentations which includes plays from great classical theatre as well as new original works. The one identifying feature which distinguishes off-off-Broadway from off-Broadway is the fact that almost all off-off-Broadway theatres are not-for-profit theatres (as opposed to the off-Broadway commercial theatre). This means that they are financed by gifts, contributions and grants. Off-Broadway theatre, as we know, is in the business of making money and is financed by investments.

Most off-off-Broadway theatres operate on annual budgets that range from $3,000.00 to over $250,000.00 annually. Yes, there is this huge disparity. The middle average annual budget (if there is such a thing, which there probably isn't) would probably be between $30,000.00 and $50,000.00.

The average production budget for a particular show is probably $1,000.00 to $1,500.00. Of course, some shows are produced for $100.00. The average production budget (if they worked it out) for a particular show in most of the theatres with large annual budgets would be in the neighborhood of $10,000.00.

There has recently been a great deal of publicity concerning negotiations between a committee representing off-off-Broadway and Actor's Equity Association concerning the showcase code and the pilot project rider often annexed to it. The conflict stems from the economic facts of off-off-Broadway life—namely, that in order to subsist, the off-off-Broadway theatres cannot pay the actors anything substantial. At the same time, Actors' Equity Association would like to know that if something good happens as a result of the original off-off-Broadway production, the original actors will be part of the new production or compensated in some manner. Of course, if the union demands become excessive enough, the new commercial producer who wants to convert the off-off-Broadway show to a Broadway or off-Broadway production, faced with having to use actors he does not want, or paying them an excessive amount of money for the privilege of not using them, may simply walk away from the project. This could hurt the author of the play and could also hurt the off-off-Broadway theatre which will share in some of the proceeds from the commercial production, usually to the extent of 1% to 5% of the net profits.

The dispute has centered around how much the cast can be paid, whether admission can be charged for the production, whether advertising may be done, how many performances may be presented under the code and the like.

The dispute continues but in the meantime, the off-off-Broadway theatres are operating under the showcase code often with the pilot project rider. The committee has come forth with a specific proposal and perhaps in the future there may be some modifications of the existing code.

Most off-off-Broadway theatres are not-for-profit corporations and, as I have stated, have an annual budget rather than a per show budget. Since they consider themselves the best theatre laboratory in the world, in many instances the non-successes are as important as the successes (if we think of success as a lot of money and a lot of people sitting in the theatre watching a particular show). Although the budgets as stated are varied, there is set forth a middle average annual budget and an average production budget for a particular show.

Resident Professional Theatre

The Resident Professional Theatre in this country operates under a contract with Actors' Equity Association designated as a L.O.R.T. contract (The League of Resident Theatres contract). Most Resident Theatres operate with an annual budget somewhere between $120,000.00 and $2 million. This does not mean that there are not Resident Theatres with much smaller and much larger budgets.

For your information, I am setting forth an annual budget for a small Resident Theatre. In addition, although most theatres do not budget each show, I am nevertheless setting forth a budget for a typical production for a student audience program for a Shakespearean play.

10   Vitally Important Odds and End

The Art of Negotiation

A brief word or two is in order at this time on the art of negotiation. One must always be conscious of the fact that there
are many factors working at the same time and that the contracts
discussed in this book are not negotiated in a vacuum. Every item
requested by either side can effect the other items that will end up
in the agreement, in that there is a good deal of give and take,
changing, exchanging, and bartering within certain defined limits. I
know that someone will, for an example, insist that they know a
producer who obtained an option for an advance payment less than
$100. Of course, there are times when options are acquired for the
payment of $1.00. Just as someone will surely tell me that in some
instances producers will only have to pay a royalty of 4% of the
gross weekly box-office receipts, or in other instances, must pay 10%
of the gross weekly box-office receipts.

I have already noted that the rare or unusual is not within the purview of this book. The give and take, change and exchange which takes place is predicated on the parties playing the game in the same ball park. If one party comes to the negotiations demanding an extreme outside the normal limits, the negotiations may be over before they start. It is not a good negotiation tactic to make unreasonable demands. If the offer is not within reason, the other party will not bid against it.

When one in this business is not totally aware of all of the ramifications of the contractual arrangements, and of what is important, it's pretty easy to become alarmed about percentage arrangements. In order to get a particular person who is important to the production to come with the show, who otherwise would not, I have at times recommended to a producer client that he should make an assignment of a part of the producer's profits to the person. That person may be the one who makes a difference between a successful show and a flop. On such occasions, I am often confronted with the comment that other producers never give anything away for this reason. On other occasions I've been told, "Why should I pay 8% to the author when an author in most agreements only gets 5% or 6%?"

There are times when one must not be fenced in by the kind of percentage arrangements that have been previously made. It is a basic axiom and one that I repeat time and again to every client I have ever represented in theatre, that: "Two percent of something can be a tremendous amount of money, and 90% of nothing is nothing." What I'm saying in effect is that the percentage amount is not as important as what you are taking the percentage of. A producer who starts with 50% of the profits of the show, even if he had to give away as much as 30% to the people who are responsible for making it a smash hit, would still do very nicely even if he ultimately ended up with only 20% of the profits. On the other hand, if the show doesn't make it, a producer who doesn't give away any of his profits but retains all 50%, ends up with 50% of nothing.

I'm not suggesting that a producer ought to go around needlessly giving away percentages of the producer's profits, nor am I suggesting that an author should be paid a larger percentage than is necessary to acquire the property. Giving does not insure a success, but not getting the right people because one won't give, may mean failure. What I am suggesting also is that the numerical percentage amount is something that shouldn't be frightening to a producer. What one is receiving in exchange for the percentage amount, and the importance of the contribution to the production, is the important consideration.

It sometimes happens that an author or a director will come to the negotiations not represented by an attorney or an agent. Whenever I am the attorney representing the producer and negotiate with another party who is not represented by someone who knows the business, I deal with the non-represented person on a different level. If I negotiate a contract on behalf of a producer, and the author is represented by an agent or an attorney, then under such circumstances I get as much for my client as I am capable of convincing the other party I should get. When I deal with someone who is not represented, I am inclined to lean over backwards to make certain that that person is treated fairly.

What can happen and sometimes does happen is that I will deal with someone on behalf of a producer, with an author for example, who is not represented by a knowledgeable party who knows the business. I arrange what I deem to be a most fair option contract. When the contract is completed but not yet signed, the author, not really understanding how fair the contract is, may give second thoughts to the arrangement and decide to consult an agent or an attorney. The next thing I know I get a telephone call and someone is telling me that he now represents the author and he wants to start the negotiations on the contract.

This is an unfair way of doing business because he would like me to now negotiate against my contract which I prepared and agreed to in an attempt to be fair when the author had no counsel. Originally, if I were negotiating against someone who did know the business, I would have taken a much firmer position and a much stronger stand in a more extreme way. For me to start negotiating with someone when the basis for the beginning of the negotiations is to be a contract which I have already established as fair, is an unreasonable imposition upon me and my client. Under such circumstances, I have to insist upon remaining firm and taking the position that there is nothing to talk about and nothing to negotiate, except upon some very minor points which might possibly have been overlooked. To begin the negotiations with the other party starting to negotiate against a contract and attempting to change a contract which I have already established as being a fair and reasonable agreement is in itself an unfair kind of dealing.

Perhaps the most important thing that one must know before one can effectively and intelligently negotiate contracts dealing with theatre, is to know what's important and what is not important, as well as the degree of importance of each particular item. Of course one must be ready to give and take but one has to know what one's giving and what one's taking and which is more important and why. The real difference between someone who negotiates well and someone who does not, rests in the ability to give in on the items which are not really important, and to hold out and stand firm for those things that are important. People who are not theatre oriented will never know what is important. One acquires this knowledge through experience.

Conflicts of Interest

It sometimes happens that a producer produces a show so that he can direct the show or act in it, or a producer produces a show which he has authored. One must always be especially careful of such an arrangement.

In the first place there will be a conflict of interest when you, as the author, sell you as the producer the rights to produce the play. Under such circumstances, when I represent an author-producer, I make certain that the producer gets the best possible deal. The reason I do this is that the producer will raise money from investors whom I feel need representation. So in a sense I look out for the investors' interests. What the author-producer does as producer affects others (the investors) and what he does as the author affects only himself. Since the producer is dealing with himself, he must do as much or more than another author would do for the producing company in the terms of the option agreement granting the rights. If the producer were negotiating at arms length with another author, there would be no question but that the producing company would end up with everything it could get and should have. There's always a question when one deals with oneself. Therefore, I make the party lean over backwards, under such circumstances, in order to be fair.

In the second place, if the producer is the director, how does he fire himself if he isn't doing a good job of directing? In fact, how does he recognize if he isn't doing a good job of directing if he is also the boss? There's always this danger when a producer directs his own production. Furthermore, the play can become very one dimensional if the producer is the director. There's something to be said for a different point of view judging the director's work. When someone tries to wear too many hats, it's very easy to lose perspective. If there is more than one producer, and if one of the producers is the director, the one who is not directing must always be in a position to replace the producer-director if things are not going well. A provision to this effect should always be incorporated into the Joint Venture agreement.

It is not unusual for an actor to assume a different name if he is acting in a show in which he is one of the producers. In doing so, the actor admits that he is doing something that he does not wish publicized. There is a feeling that it does not look good for an actor to have to produce the show to get the job.

There are drawbacks to a producer hiring himself as an actor, for the producer ought always to be in a position to replace even the star of the show if things are not going as they should.

Obviously there are some striking exceptions which may be called to my attention. There are indeed several famous names in the theatre who were equally competent as actors, directors, and producers, and on occasions perform all three roles at the same time. It's just not usual nor advisable. Most of us will do well if we can handle any one of these three jobs in a competent professional way.

Package Deals

You should also be very sceptical of a package deal if it is offered to you. It sometimes happens that for whatever reason, someone wants to sponsor a particular person and offers you a property if you use a particular person as the director. You may on the other hand be offered all or a large part of the financing if you use a particular actress. There is nothing wrong with one of the people you cast bringing in a sum of money, but if the reason for the casting is the money, then you are making a mistake. As a producer you must never abdicate your responsibility of selecting the best people for the right reasons. To do a play badly simply because it was easier to get the money that way will not only mean a great waste of your time and energy but will contribute to a reputation for expediency rather than judgment and taste.

The League of Off-Broadway Theatres and Producers

A most appropriate and useful way in which an industry may solve its problems is the formation of a group in which persons and businesses connected with that industry meet to discuss their common problems and to find a way to solve them by frank and open discussion. Such is the case of the League of Off-Broadway Theatres and Producers. Nine years ago the League was formed by the theatre owners and producers operating off-Broadway to perpetuate the off-Broadway theatre. They joined together to resolve the common problems which had been confronting them. The League of off-Broadway Theatres and Producers through the years has established a labor relationship with Actors' Equity Association in which the parties have negotiated an employment contract covering the off-Broadway theatre. In addition the League serves as an information conduit regarding activities which take place, and registers the dates of opening night performances so that there are no conflicts within the off-Broadway theatre. It is most advisable that a producer who is seriously interested in producing off-Broadway become a member of this organization. Membership may be had by telephoning the League of Off-Broadway Theatres and Producers.

Ethics — Honesty

It's not just a matter of ethics, but honesty is good business. Bear this in mind in all of your theatre dealings.

It sometimes happens that someone who is producing an off-Broadway show gets the mistaken idea that he can accomplish certain things by being devious. Sometimes the fervor to do a show becomes so great that one is willing to cut corners and do things that one would otherwise not think of doing. It's true that "the show must go on," but it must go on right. I have on occasion had clients try to use me in their devious dishonest maneuvers. For an example, there have been occasions when someone will negotiate for something they do not have the money to pay for, and will try to impose upon me to call the other party to tell them that I'm holding the money. Of course, if I'm not going to be dishonest myself, and I'm not, then I'm not going to permit a client to use me to assist in his dishonesty. If you haven't raised all of the money necessary to release the funds to you to start the show, then don't start using the money and don't start the show. It's not only dishonest, it's bad business. Don't misrepresent to someone that you've signed that star unless you have signed that star. It's not only dishonest, it's bad business. Don't misrepresent by saying that you've raised $27,000 of the budget if you have only raised $12,000. It's not only dishonest, it's bad business.

You must know, of course, that you are going into a very risky business. When the chance of a successful off-Broadway production is something like one out of twelve, you realize that the odds are against you. Even that one out of twelve which is successful may not prove to be the kind of a smash hit that will return tremendous amounts of money to you. There are all kinds of reasons for wanting to produce a show, and chances are that the money is not the sole motivation. If it is, then it would be easy to find other businesses with a greater chance of success.

The theatre business is a small family. If you are serious about becoming a producer, then you are not in the business to simply get one show produced, but intend to produce other shows. Your reputation will follow you in everything you do. You will be known in this little family for what you really are. It's just as easy if not easier to be honest in your dealings, not just because it's ethical, but because it's good business. I know the "successful" producers in the business who are not honest. Everyone in the business knows them. They are not successful because of their dishonesty. They are not respected, they are not appreciated, they are not good businessmen. Play square, not just because it's the right thing to do, but also because it's good business.

I'm often asked, "Aren't theatre people immoral or dishonest?" This question of course is utter nonsense. Theatre people are moral and immoral, honest and dishonest, just like other people. The difference is that theatre people have different problems. Of course, the implication is that all people have problems. For the most part, my friends and clients in theatre are considerate, intelligent, bright, sensitive people.

Good Producing

A show, more than almost any other business, is a team project. Until you've been in the business and see how things happen, it's hard to understand that everything and everyone is dependent on everyone else in the production. Of course, when the actors are on stage they influence each other, but I am talking about something more than that. There's an interaction between the actors and the stage manager; between the director and the actors; between the actors and the company manager; between the stage manager and the producer; between the producer and the general manager; between the attorney and the producer; between the press agent and the actors; and so on.

If you have a successful production, as the producer, don't break your arm patting your back because you didn't do it by yourself. Probably the one thing that you did that you want to take the least credit for, but that may have conributed the most to the show, is that you have selected very good people in each of the areas of their endeavor and turned over the reins to them. A good producer doesn't have to be a person who does or even knows how to do all of the jobs in a production. A good producer can be a person who knows how to select all of the important people who will do their jobs in a remarkable fashion, and in selecting the people, to select those whose chemistry works together, who vibrate on the same wave length, and who together make magic. When that marvelous, spellbinding thing happens, and everything seems to fall in place and work, you will wake up one morning and have a hit on your hands.

Middle Theatres in New York

Some mention should be made of "middle theatres." You will remember that an off-Broadway theatre is a theatre outside a certain geographical area in New York City having more than 299 seats. There are some theatres which are neither Broadway theatres nor can they come within the definition of an off-Broadway theatre as defined in the Actors' Equity Minimum Basic Contract, which is the commonly used definition. These theatres have acquired the name "middle theatres," and though the name seems to indicate that they are something between Broadway and off-Broadway, the differences in the various theatres is sometimes great.

There are, for an example, theatres outside the Broadway area containing more than 299 seats.

There are also theatres within the Broadway area containing 299 seats or less.

There is now another classification which technically comes within the definition of a Broadway theatre except that it contains a smaller number of seats than the usual Broadway theatre. There is a theatre within the Broadway area with less than 500 seats and most Broadway theatres contain 900 seats or more. Even though the theatre is in the Broadway area, if it contains only 499 seats it cannot and ought not have the usual Broadway contract conditions as a theatre with 950 seats.

To confuse the situation even more, some of the theatres are not "theatres" in that they are operating under a cabaret license (which is different than a theatre license) and are "cabarets" rather than "theatres." Cabarets are supposed to serve drinks and food. What has happened is that they do not always do this so that although the license is different, one would be hard-put sometimes to distinguish the difference between cabarets and theatres from one's observation of the premises.

The productions in middle theatres are eligible for Tony Awards and the other benefits of a Broadway house. Each show in each theatre must negotiate separate union terms which could vary. There are no fixed standard union contracts.

Before signing a lease or license agreement to go into a middle theatre, a producer would be wise to make certain that he understands all of the arrangements with various unions so that there is no question as to his obligations. Bear in mind that Actors' Equity is just one of the unions any new theatre must make its peace with. Since each theatre arrangement varies it is impossible to delineate exactly what the union requirements are. Just make certain you know what you are getting yourself into.

OFF-OFF-BROADWAY THEATRE BUDGET

July 1, 1975—June 30, 1976

I.   INCOME

A.	Theatre Rental	$ 7664.00
B.	Ticket Sales	
	Cash	10625.00
	T.D.F.	2000.00
C.	Concession	595.00
D.	High School Programs	1988.00
E.	Program Advertising	800.00
F.	Subscriptions	6000.00
G.	Classes — Tuition	1500.00
H.	Directing Festival Registration	900.00
I.	Insurance Rebate	1000.00
J.	Loan Repayment	360.00
K.	Private Contributions	10000.00
L.	Benefits	5000.00
	Total 1975-76 Income	$48432.00

II.   EXPENDITURES

A.   Operating Expenses

Rent (12 mths. @ $600. per mth)	$ 7200.00
Con Edison (12 mths @ $300. per mth)	3600.00
Telephone (12 mths @ $100. per mth)	1200.00
Insurance	1000.00
Dues/Publications	60.00
Transportation	150.00
Permits	150.00
Equipment (donated)	
Maintenance Supplies	250.00
Plant and Equipment Repairs	500.00
Office Supplies	100.00
Postage	300.00

Concession	300.00
Total Operating Expenses	$14810.00

B. Salaries and Fees (September 1 through June 30 = 44 weeks)

Artistic Director ($200 weekly)	$ 8800.00
Production Coordinator/Secretary ($150 weekly)	6600.00
Legal Fees	1000.00
Accounting Fee	600.00
Artists and Technicians — Part Time	5900.00
F.I.C.A.	900.00
Total Salaries and Fees	$23800.00

C. Production Expenses

Five Main Productions

Sets, Costumes, Lights, Sound, Props	$2500.00
Programs/Tickets	600.00
Flyers/Postage	750.00
Advertising	1000.00

11:00 Series — Two Productions

Sets, Costumes, Lights, Sound, Props	200.00
Programs/Tickets	100.00
Flyers/Postage	300.00
Advertising	300.00

Spring Festival

Sets, Costumes, Lights, Sound, Props	125.00
Programs/Tickets	100.00
Flyers/Postage	150.00
Advertising	150.00

Fall Festival

Sets, Costumes, Lights, Sound, Props	125.00
Programs/Tickets	100.00
Flyers/Postage	150.00
Advertising	150.00
Total Production Expenses	$6800.00

D. High School Programs
      Fall Institute (Programs, Flyers, Postage) $100.00
      Spring Festival (Programs, Flyers, Postage)   200.00

                        Total High School Prog. $300.00

E. Promotion/Fund Raising
      Signs, Photos, Blow-ups $ 300.00
      Subscription Brochure/Mailing   600.00
      Benefits — Food and Entertainmnt
         (donated by Board of Directors)
      Advertising (Casting, Class, Theatre Rent)   700.00
      Press Releases/Mailing   350.00

                        Total Promotion $1950.00

F. 1974-75 Deficit $ 1000.00

                        Total Deficit   1000.00

                Total Expenses 1975-76 $48660.00

III. EARNINGS GAP
    Total Expenses $48660.00
    Total Income   48432.00
    Deficit   — $ 228.00

RESIDENT THEATRE COMPANY BUDGET
1975-76

Income:

Ticket Sales	$176000.00
Less Box Office Commission	3800.00
	$172200.00
Rental Income	10000.00
City/County Grant	38250.00
Angel Campaign	20000.00
Follies	10000.00
Second fundraising event	7500.00
Corporate Campaign	102500.00
	$178250.00
Total Income	$360450.00

Expenses:
Administrative Costs

Salaries	$ 60500.00
Payroll costs	4000.00
Operations	14500.00
Advertising and Promotion	46000.00
	$125000.00

Production costs

Artistic Salaries	$ 92100.00
Technical Salaries	41500.00
Payroll related costs	18500.00
Sets, props, costumes	26000.00
Electrics	2000.00

Travel		6000.00
Royalties		7500.00
Stage Manager's Misc.		2000.00
		$195600.00
Theatre Occupancy		39850.00
	Total Costs	$360450.00

RESIDENT THEATRE COMPANY
Budget for Shakespearean Student Audience Program

Expenses:

Artistic Salaries	$13965.00
Technical Salaries	2174.00
Administrative Salaries	1884.00
Payroll related costs	2500.00
Advertising and Promotion	3000.00
Study Guides	500.00
Operations	1000.00
Sets, Props, Costumes	5400.00
Electrics and Sound	600.00
Contractual Travel	1000.00
Stage Manager's Misc.	400.00
Occupancy of Theatre	4500.00
Total Costs	$36923.00

Income:

Student Matinees (14)	$20000.00
Public Performances (including Students)	15000.00
Total Income	$35000.00
Deficit	$ 1923.00

ESTIMATED PRODUCTION BUDGET
FOR 499 SEAT THEATRE
(Middle Theatre)
1 SET—CAST OF 8—2 UNDERSTUDIES

Expenses:

Scenery, Props., etc.		$4500.00
Costumes		2000.00
Electrics, sound (rentals and purchases)		2000.00
	Total	$8500.00

Fees:

Director		$1500.00
Designers — Set, Costumes, Lighting		6000.00
	Total	$7500.00

Rehearsals:

Salaries — cast (8) — 8 x $285 (4 weeks)		$ 9120.00
understudies (2) 2 x $285 (2 weeks)		1140.00
Stage manager — 1 x $420 (5 weeks)		2100.00
Assistant stage manager — 1 x $335 (4 weeks)		1340.00
Press Agent 1 x $350 (5 weeks)		1750.00
Company Manager 1 x $350 (4 weeks)		1400.00
The crew		1500.00
	Total	$18350.00

Advertising:

Newspapers, etc.		$ 9000.00
Photographs and signs		1800.00
Press Agent's expenses		250.00
	Total	$11050.00

Estimated Production Expenses
(Exclusive of Bonds, Previews
and/or Out-of-Town Losses)

Audit	$ 1000.00
Legal costs	6000.00
Legal advertising	1000.00
Office (6 x $400)	2400.00
General Manager	2500.00
Payroll Tax (12% of rehearsal expenses)	2202.00
Insurance	1000.00
Employee welfare	1000.00
Scripts	250.00
Casting	750.00
Rehearsal halls and related expenses	2000.00
Transportation and haulage	1000.00
Preliminary Box Office and Theatre expenses	1300.00
Opening night expenses	600.00
Tickets	550.00
Total	$23,552.00

Bonds:

Actors Equity Association (including pension bond)	$ 25220.00
Press Agent and Manager's (ATPAM) Bond	6400.00
Total	$ 31620.00
Advance to Theatres	$ 12000.00

Total Estimated Production Costs	$112572.00
Reserve	$ 27428.00
Total	$140000.00

ESTIMATED WEEKLY OPERATING BUDGET

499 SEAT THEATRE

(Middle Theatre)

(Computed with Gross Receipts—$19,000.00)

EXPENSES:

Salaries and Royalties

Cast (8 x $285)	$2280.00
Understudies (2 x $285)	570.00
General and Company Managers	
(1 x $400) and (1 x $350)	750.00
Company Crew	150.00
Wardrobe and Dressers	125.00
Press Agent	350.00
Royalties (10%)	1900.00
	$6125.00

Publicity:

Advertising	$4000.00
Press Agent's expenses	50.00
	$4050.00

Departmental:

Property	$ 25.00
Electrical and Sound	50.00
Wardrobe	100.00
Stage Manager	25.00
Carpenter	50.00
Rentals	250.00
Office Expenses	400.00
Audit	150.00

Legal	100.00
Box Office Help, Theatre Rent and expenses	6000.00
Payroll Tax	500.00
Insurance	150.00
Employee Welfare	75.00
League dues	25.00
Equity Dinners	50.00
	$ 7950.00
Rehearsal Expenses	$ 61.00
Vacation	114.00
New York City rent tax	250.00
Long Distance telephone and telegraph	100.00
Miscellaneous	350.00
Total Expenses	$19000.00

Break even at $19,000.00. Approximately 46.4% of capacity if scaled to gross $41,000.00.